TIME OF MY LIFE

A Play

by Alan Ayckbourn

samuelfrench.co.uk

THINKING ABOUT PERFORMING A SHOW?

There are thousands of plays and musicals available to perform from Samuel French right now, and applying for a licence is easier and more affordable than you might think

---

From classic plays to brand new musicals, from monologues to epic dramas, there are shows for everyone.

Plays and musicals are protected by copyright law so if you want to perform them, the first thing you'll need is a licence. This simple process helps support the playwright by ensuring they get paid for their work, and means that you'll have the documents you need to stage the show in public.

Not all our shows are available to perform all the time, so it's important to check and apply for a licence before you start rehearsals or commit to doing the show.

LEARN MORE & FIND THOUSANDS OF SHOWS

Browse our full range of plays and musicals and find out more about how to license a show

www.samuelfrench.co.uk/perform

Talk to the friendly experts in our Licensing team for advice on choosing a show, and help with licensing

plays@samuelfrench.co.uk   020 7387 9373

Acting Editions

BORN TO PERFORM

Playscripts designed from the ground up to work the way you do in rehearsal, performance and study

---

Larger, clearer text for easier reading

Wider margins for notes

Performance features such as character and props lists, sound and lighting cues, and more

---

+ CHOOSE A SIZE AND STYLE TO SUIT YOU

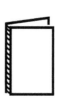

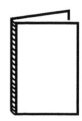

STANDARD EDITION

Our regular paperback book at our regular size

SPIRAL-BOUND EDITION

The same size as the Standard Edition, but with a sturdy, easy-to-fold, easy-to-hold spiral-bound spine

LARGE EDITION

A4 size and spiral bound, with larger text and a blank page for notes opposite every page of text. Perfect for technical and directing use

**Other plays by ALAN AYCKBOURN
published by Samuel French**

Absent Friends

Absurd Person Singular

Arrivals and Departures

Awaking Beauty

Bedroom Farce

Body Language

Callisto 5

The Champion of Paribanou

A Chorus of Disapproval

Comic Potential

Communicating Doors

Confusions

A Cut in the Rates

Dreams from a Summer House

Drowning on Dry Land

Ernie's Incredible Illucinations

Family Circles

Farcicals

My Very Own Story

My Wonderful Day

Neighbourhood Watch

The Norman Conquests: Table Manners; Living Together;
Round and Round the Garden

Private Fears in Public Places

Relatively Speaking

The Revengers' Comedies

RolePlay

Roundelay

Season's Greetings

Sisterly Feelings

A Small Family Business

Snake in the Grass

Suburban Strains

Sugar Daddies

Taking Steps

Ten Times Table

Things We Do for Love

This Is Where We Came In

Time and Time Again

Time of My Life

Tons of Money (revised)

Way Upstream

Wildest Dreams

Wolf at the Door

Woman in Mind

A Word from Our Sponsor

FIND PERFECT PLAYS TO PERFORM AT
www.samuelfrench.co.uk/perform

ABOUT THE AUTHOR

Alan Ayckbourn has worked in theatre as a playwright and director for over fifty years, rarely if ever tempted by television or film, which perhaps explains why he continues to be so prolific. To date he has written more than 79 plays, many one act plays and a large amount of work for the younger audience. His work has been translated into over 35 languages, is performed on stage and television throughout the world and has won countless awards.

Major successes include: *Relatively Speaking, How the Other Half Loves, Absurd Person Singular, Bedroom Farce, A Chorus of Disapproval,* and *The Norman Conquests.* In recent years, there have been revivals of *Season's Greetings* and *A Small Family Business* at the National Theatre, in the West End *Absent Friends, A Chorus of Disapproval, Relatively Speaking* and *How the Other Half Loves.* In 2015, Chichester mounted a very successful revival of *Way Upstream.*

Artistic Director of the Stephen Joseph Theatre from 1972 – 2009 where almost all his plays have been first staged, he continues to direct his latest new work there. In recent years, he has been inducted into American Theatre's Hall of Fame, received the 2010 Critics' Circle Award for Services to the Arts and became the first British playwright to receive both Olivier and Tony Special Lifetime Achievement Awards. He was knighted in 1997 for services to the theatre.

Image credit: Andrew Higgins.

AUTHOR'S NOTE

After a lifetime of playwriting (I first started as an unpublished writer at the age of ten!) my career has moved steadily forward from the status of untried tyro through to establishment figure to ageing experimentalist!

The work has reflected this. From the early tried and tested plays, (*Relatively Speaking, How the Other Half Loves, The Norman Conquests*, etc.) which thankfully people still seem happy to produce and come to see, through the middle period, larger scale so called "social" pieces (*Man of the Moment, A Chorus of Disapproval*) to the more recent smaller scale departures such as *Private Fears in Public Places, Snake in the Grass and Haunting Julia*, I have continued to experiment with shape and form, whilst I hope continuing to deepen my characters.

Throughout this, though, I have always needed to remind myself of the overriding prime directive drummed into me at an early age by my mentor, Stephen Joseph, that above all else a playwright is a storyteller.

To keep an audience in their seats you need to involve them in a constantly unfolding series of unexpected twists and turns. These can, of course, be the narrative of the story itself as in *Relatively Speaking* or, as with *Woman in Mind* say, through the psychological development of the characters.

One of the nicest things people can ever say to me, coming out of a new play for the first time of seeing it, is "Well, I never saw THAT coming!"

Alan Ayckbourn

MUSIC USE NOTE

Licensees are solely responsible for obtaining formal written permission from copyright owners to use copyrighted music in the performance of this play and are strongly cautioned to do so. If no such permission is obtained by the licensee, then the licensee must use only original music that the licensee owns and controls. Licensees are solely responsible and liable for all music clearances and shall indemnify the copyright owners of the play(s) and their licensing agent, Samuel French, against any costs, expenses, losses and liabilities arising from the use of music by licensees. Please contact the appropriate music licensing authority in your territory for the rights to any incidental music.

IMPORTANT BILLING AND CREDIT REQUIREMENTS

If you have obtained performance rights to this title, please refer to your licensing agreement for important billing and credit requirements.

First performed at the Stephen Joseph Theatre in the Round, Scarborough, on 21st April 1992, with the following cast:

GERRY	Russell Dixon
LAURA	Collette O'Neill
GLYN	Richard Garnett
ADAM	Stephen Mapes
STEPHANIE	Karen Drury
MAUREEN	Sophie Heyman
CALVINU	
TUTO	
AGGI	Terence Booth
DINKA	
BENGIE	

Directed by Alan Ayckbourn
Designed by Roger Glossop
Lighting by Mick Hughes

Subsequently performed at the Vaudeville Theatre, London,on 3rd August 1993, with the following cast:

GERRY	Anton Rodgers
LAURA	Gwen Taylor
GLYN	Richard Garnett
ADAM	Stephen Mapes
STEPHANIE	Karen Drury
MAUREEN	Sophie Heyman
CALVINU	
TUTO	
AGGI	Terence Booth
DINKA	
BENGIE	

Directed by Alan Ayckbourn
Designed by Roger Glossop
Lighting by Mick Hughes

CHARACTERS

GERRY, a business man
LAURA, his wife
GLYN, their elder son
ADAM, their younger son
STEPHANIE, Glyn's wife
MAUREEN

CALVINU, a restaurant owner ⎫
TUTO, head waiter ⎪
AGGI, a waiter ⎬ played by the same actor
DINKA, another waiter ⎪
BENGIE, yet another waiter ⎭

Scene—Calvinu's restaurant, the Essa de Calvi
Time—past, present and future

ACT I

The restaurant Essa de Calvi.

The restaurant could be Greek, it could be Italian, even French or Spanish. It is none of these. It is whatever we decide to make it. It's a family concern, shabby but clean. Slightly under-lit. Distant piped music of indeterminate ethnic origin is heard from time to time. There can be several tables on view depending on the space available. Only three need be used, though: two "twos" – window tables – set apart at a distance, one downstage left (for **ADAM** *and* **MAUREEN***) and one downstage right (for* **GLYN** *and* **STEPHANIE***) and a large central table set for a party of six. There are entrances upstage centre, left and right. At the start there is a family dinner in progress at the main table. The other two are empty. The meal is all but over. It is around 10.30 p.m. on Saturday, 18th January. Evidence of the supper litters the table. Used coffee cups, dirty plates, sweet-papers, full ashtrays and half empty liqueur glasses. Also, evidence of gift wrapping paper, suggesting that someone has had a birthday.*

At either end of the table sit the parents, **LAURA** *and* **GERRY***, both in their fifties. He is a successful, self-made business man. Originally a builder, he has diversified and managed to weather economic storms and recessions through a combination of astuteness and ruthlessness. There is no doubt that, visibly at least, he is very much the head of the family. A man who rarely if ever expects his words or actions to be questioned. But he hasn't achieved this single-handedly.* **LAURA***, his wife, is also a force to be reckoned with, despite the fact that her*

*profile, publicly, may suggest she exists purely to support
her husband. But as so often in such partnerships,
she has played a vital if largely unsung role in her
husband's success. She is just as astute and every bit
as determined. Though they are both dressed for their
evening out,* **GERRY** *is more casually attired than his
wife. Around and under* **LAURA**'s *chair are some of her
birthday presents, now unwrapped. A large mantelpiece
clock, a macramé flower basket holder and a slim volume
of poems.* **LAURA** *is currently holding her other present,
a pair of not unacceptable but modest "craft" ear-rings.*
GERRY *and* **LAURA** *are a well-matched couple, and if
their ambitions and drives have diminished slightly over
the years and given way to a certain complacency and
self-satisfaction, the pair are quite clearly, as they say,
still on the board and in play – especially so far as their
dealings with their own family are concerned. The closest
of these, their two sons,* **GLYN** *and* **ADAM**, *are also present.*
GLYN, *in his late twenties, is at first glance perhaps very
much his father's son, a second version of his parent.
But he has lived for too long in* **GERRY**'s *shadow, has
been compared unfavourably to his father just once too
often, has tried to compete with an over-competitive
parent and failed. He has been groomed to take over
the family business, but it is unlikely that the firm will
survive his father's death. He has charm but little of his
father's drive or ambition. Across the table from him
sits his wife,* **STEPHANIE**. *In her mid-twenties, she has
borne him one child and, as a result of recent emotional
upheavals in her marriage, has worn less well than she
should have done for someone reasonably comfortably
off and with few material worries. One can only assume
that in marrying* **GLYN** *she may have hoped she was
marrying the father. She has since learnt better. Where
she sought strength she has found weakness; instead of
decisiveness nothing but vacillation and uncertainty.*
STEPHANIE *is seated next to her younger brother-in-law,*
ADAM, *who is the apple of his mother's eye. In his early*

twenties, he is a nervous, uncoordinated windmill of a boy and in gatherings such as these hopelessly out of his depth. One of the reasons ADAM *is more anxious than usual tonight is due to the behaviour of his own partner seated across the table,* MAUREEN. *She is very much the outsider. She is* ADAM*'s new girlfriend and this is her first meeting with the family. She is very drunk. This has taken the form of a sort of glazed, fixed smiling trance. The room is evidently revolving for her quite rapidly, the floor rocking up and down at regular intervals. Whatever small contribution she might have made earlier to the evening is now reduced to a loud, regular hiccup. Apart from the occasional nervous glance from* ADAM, *the others have all chosen to act as if she doesn't exist.*

But now the party is nearly at an end. From a distance, they are a jolly group enjoying each other's company. After all, it is LAURA*'s birthday and no one would want to spoil that.*

Around the table, coffee pot in hand, flits TUTO, *one of several waiters we shall meet. They all have a marked resemblance, unsurprisingly, since they are all related in various ways to the head of the family and owner of the restaurant,* ERNESTO CALVINU. TUTO *is eternally cheerful and happy to serve.*

At the start, there are two conversations in progress, one between GERRY *and* GLYN *and another between* LAURA *and* STEPHANIE, *all talking across each other.* ADAM *and* MAUREEN *remain very much spectators.* LAURA *is holding the ear-rings, evidently a present from* GLYN *and* STEPHANIE.

The following conversation between LAURA *and* STEPHANIE *occurs simultaneously with the conversation between* GERRY *and* GLYN *on page 6. At some stage during the combined exchange,* TUTO *serves coffee and says his dialogue on page 8. The conversations cease when* MAUREEN *rushes out of the room on page 8.*

LAURA *(to* STEPHANIE*)* ...they're so unusual. That's what I love about them. I don't think I've seen anything like them before. Not even in Crete.

STEPHANIE No, as I say, there's this woman we met at the nursery school, she's just started up. She's working from home but she was trained in jewellery making. She's fully trained. But she gave it up to have children but now they're at school she's just starting up again on her own from home...

LAURA I've not seen anything like them anywhere. I think they're just lovely. I think I'll probably go to bed in them...

STEPHANIE They suit you, I thought they'd suit you. They're your colour...

LAURA They are. They're exactly my colour. I wear this colour all the time...

STEPHANIE Yes, I've seen you wearing that colour... You've got that necklace that's not dissimilar, too, haven't you...? You know, the one you sometimes wear with—

LAURA Yes, I have. That's what I mean. I think they're the same stones. Semi-precious...

STEPHANIE Semi-precious, yes—

LAURA I prefer semi-precious, sometimes, you know. For certain occasions. I mean if you're just on your own, slopping around the house. You want to look good for yourself but you don't necessarily want to look that special. I mean for that you want semi-precious, you don't necessarily want precious, do you?

STEPHANIE No. I feel exactly the same. I know you're not supposed to—

LAURA Well, a diamond. A beautiful diamond. That takes a lot of beating...

STEPHANIE Oh well, a diamond... We're not talking about diamonds—

LAURA And sapphires, I love sapphires. Gerry gave me a sapphire bracelet when we first moved to Forest Road...

STEPHANIE I know, I've seen it on you. Oh, I covet that.

LAURA Well, God knows what it cost him. A damn sight more than we could afford in those days. But I love it to death. I wear it a lot...it was the first bit of real jewellery I ever owned.

STEPHANIE Yes—

LAURA You know what I mean, real jewellery...?

STEPHANIE Yes, yes—

LAURA I'd have worn it tonight, only—

STEPHANIE I love that bracelet—

LAURA I wear it a lot. Mind you, I'll wear these a lot, I think... I can see me wearing them a lot...

STEPHANIE I'll give you her address...

LAURA They're lovely... They'll do especially for daytime...

STEPHANIE Well, they're meant for daytime, really... I'll let you have her address. She lives quite near us...

LAURA Lovely, look at the light in them...

STEPHANIE They look very good in daylight. They're daytime jewellery, really. But I think they're unusual, aren't they?

LAURA They're certainly unusual...

STEPHANIE All her stuff's unusual. She does shoe bags as well. I've got her card. I'll give it to you—

LAURA Rubies. I quite like rubies, too. For certain occasions.

STEPHANIE Yes. I'm not so sure about rubies.

The following conversation between GERRY *and* GLYN
occurs simultaneously with the conversation between
LAURA *and* STEPHANIE, *above.*

GERRY *(to* GLYN*)* ...there's no use him complaining about
deadlines and what should have been done then and what
wasn't done when it should have been done – he has to
understand we're talking today—

GLYN Yes, yes, yes—

GERRY we're not talking twenty years ago when a supplier
was prepared to wait six, nine months – a year sometimes
before he got paid.

GLYN No, no—

GERRY Most of the fellers we deal with nowadays, they're not
prepared to wait at all—

GLYN No, no, no—

GERRY because they, in turn, have got cash-flow problems just
like anyone else—

GLYN Yes, yes...

GERRY – just as we have—

GLYN Yes...

GERRY and they're not just reaching for things off shelves, not
these days—

GLYN No, no...

GERRY they can't afford it any more than we can—

GLYN No, no. Well, I said to him—

GERRY they're having to pay for them, cash up front—

GLYN Yes, I explained to him—

GERRY Those are the basic facts of life. He has to understand
them...

GLYN Well, I phoned him three times and—

GERRY I mean, let's put it this way. What he's failing to appreciate
— what he is quite transparently failing to appreciate — is
the amount of *hidden* subsidy he's getting from us — every
time he withholds an account—

GLYN Yes, I know, this is what I was—

GERRY that he has previously — let me finish — that he has
previously in writing and technically, legally bindingly
agreed to pay...

GLYN Well, it's easy to say that but—

GERRY I'll talk to him. Don't worry, I'll talk to him tomorrow.
He's the same as his father, I knew his father and he used
to try it on. Eighteen months I had to wait for him, once—

GLYN Yes, I know.

GERRY Eighteen months and then he asked me, would I mind
overlooking the interest. I told him get — I told him—

GLYN I know, I know—

GERRY I mean, we were talking three or four hundred quid
in interest—

GLYN Yes—

GERRY That was a lot of money—

GLYN It was—

GERRY in those days...

GLYN Quite.

GERRY Times have changed, but it's still no different today—

GLYN No.

GERRY More brandy? Another brandy?

GLYN ⎱   ⎰ No thanks, Dad, we need to be – Baby-sitter,
     ⎰(together)⎱   you know...
ADAM ⎰   ⎱ (softly, across to MAUREEN) You all right?

MAUREEN *nods miserably, but by way of a reply can only hiccup. She is evidently feeling very sick.*

Simultaneously with the above exchanges, TUTO *circles the table offering fresh coffee.* STEPHANIE, MAUREEN, GLYN *and* ADAM *all decline when asked.* LAURA *and* GERRY *both say yes.*

TUTO *(to* LAURA*)* More coffee? Madama? ...Yes? Good. Delicious coffee, with my own nuts. Yes? *(To* MAUREEN*)* Madametta? More coffee? No? *(To* STEPHANIE*)* Madama? Some lovely coffee? No? You break my heart. I cry all night. *(To* GERRY *)* Mr Stratton? Yes? Yes. Of course. *(To* GLYN*)* Seerar? No? No coffee? *(To* ADAM*)* Seerar? Of course. Coffee. No? No coffee. Beautiful coffee. I grow it myself... *(Back to* MAUREEN, *whom he obviously fancies)* Madametta? Please? No? Some liqueur? Crème de menthe? Some Crouscac? Grown in my village, very rich, very sweet. Just for the lady?

MAUREEN *looks green.*

No Crouscac? Some more sweet? Smooliboos? That is sugar melted with rum and cream and baked with eggs in a meringue case with a beautiful outside of chocolate and rich fresh cream and *glacé* fruits. Delicious.

MAUREEN's *stomach turns over.*

Some trickletasse? This is delicious tart with treacle and cream mixed with passion fruit, fresh strawberries and Armagnac—

MAUREEN *rises suddenly from the table and makes a dash for the door. This has the effect of stopping the other conversations.*

Madametta...?

ADAM *(rising, alarmed)* Maureen... *(Hastily, to the others)* Excuse me...

He exits after **MAUREEN**.

TUTO *(slightly bemused)* Madametta, she is...?

LAURA *(rather tight-lipped)* Madametta is slightly under the weather, I'm afraid.

TUTO Ah! I tell Seerar Calvinu...

TUTO goes off after them.

A brief silence at the table.

LAURA Oh dear, oh dear, oh dear...

GERRY Yes—

LAURA Where does he find them? Where does that boy find them?

GERRY *(magnanimously)* Well—

LAURA No, seriously, Gerry, there are dozens of girls who'd be glad of him. Literally hundreds walking about out there. They'd give their right legs for a boy like Adam...

STEPHANIE It's not always that straightforward though, is it...?

LAURA It's perfectly straightforward...

STEPHANIE Not always—

LAURA I'm sorry, I don't see the problem, I'm sorry.

STEPHANIE It's meeting them, you have to get to meet them first, don't you? I don't think Adam meets that many girls, does he, Glyn?

GLYN No, I don't think he meets that many—

LAURA He could do if he wanted to – I don't care what they say, even today it's still easier for a man. I mean Glyn met you, didn't he?

STEPHANIE Yes, he did—

LAURA I mean Glyn's never had trouble meeting girls...

STEPHANIE He hasn't—

LAURA There we are, then. No, the trouble with Adam is they meet him. He doesn't have to look, they come out of the woodwork and seek him out, like that one did. He's a sitting target for every little tart in the district.

STEPHANIE Now, I don't think that's very fair—

TUTO *hurries through busily, calling another waiter, who is unseen.*

TUTO Bengie! Bengie! Chella bucketti. Ser madametta machosessa re-gorgettor. *("BENGIE! BENGIE! Fetch a bucket. The young lady has been sick in the Gents." To the others)* It's OK. She's OK...

He goes off.

GERRY Shouldn't someone see how she is?

LAURA She's all right, Adam's with her...

GERRY He's not going to be much use, is he? Not if she's bolted herself in the Ladies...

LAURA She'll manage, it's her own fault. She was knocking them back like a goldfish... She had that champagne cocktail down in one gulp to start with, then she had three glasses of the Chablis—

GLYN That was excellent...

GERRY Yes, it was—

LAURA and at least four refills to my knowledge of that red I never touched...

GERRY Australian that. Good, wasn't it?

GLYN Australian? I thought it was Australian...

LAURA And on top of that she had all that Benedictine, or whatever it was—

STEPHANIE What were you doing, counting her?

LAURA I couldn't help but noticing, could I? I'm surprised none of you did—

GERRY We noticed—

LAURA Not until it was too late, you didn't—

GERRY Well—

LAURA I say I don't know where he finds them.

GERRY It's all right, it won't last. You know Adam...

STEPHANIE It might. How do we know it won't?

LAURA I hope to God it doesn't... I fear for that boy, sometimes.

GERRY He's not a kid now, Laura. He's twenty-four years old... It's his choice.

LAURA He's twenty-three. He's not twenty-four till next October. And I'm saying, it wasn't his choice—

GLYN Twenty-three's a grown man...

LAURA Maybe for you it was, for Adam at that age he's still finding himself. And he needs protecting from girls like that, who are just out for the main chance—

STEPHANIE I think you're being really unfair to her, you know...

GLYN Nobody protected me from girls like that...

LAURA Well, you. You both went into your marriage with your eyes open. Nothing I could do about that. You had to find out for yourselves. Well, you've been through the tunnel, you've both come out the other side, sadder but wiser and with a bit of luck you've learnt your lesson, I hope, and you'll know better next time. But with Adam, it's different. He needs help, he can't cope with these things on his own. He never could.

STEPHANIE He's going to have to one day, isn't he?

LAURA Not while I'm around. I'm amazed at you, Stephanie. I thought as a mother yourself, you might understand how I feel.

STEPHANIE *holds back her reply.*

BENGIE, *a younger waiter who speaks no English, hurries through anxiously.*

BENGIE *(calling behind him)* ...er goopini muckletracker, san? *("The mop in the cleaning cupboard, you say?" To the others)'*Scoos.

BENGIE *exits.*

STEPHANIE I think I'd better see if she needs some help.

LAURA *(rising)* No, it's all right, I'll go. I need to powder my nose, anyway.

STEPHANIE Let me know if I can.

LAURA She'll be right as rain. She just needs her head in a bucket... And quite frankly while we're at it, I do think a son of mine can do a lot better for himself than a hairdresser...

LAURA *goes out.*

GERRY I don't think, somehow, that one's gone down too well with your mother.

STEPHANIE She's fine. She was just very nervous, that's all...

GERRY Nervous?

STEPHANIE Not surprising, meeting you lot. I was nervous...

GLYN What's wrong with being a hairdresser...?

STEPHANIE Nothing wrong with being a hairdresser...

GERRY You know your mother...

STEPHANIE I was a shop assistant, I'm amazed you let me through the front door...

GLYN Ah well. It was only me you were marrying. Didn't matter so much, did it? And it was a very high-class shop, after all...

STEPHANIE I only wish she'd leave Adam alone. He has to find out for himself, doesn't he?

GERRY I've heard a rumour they're closing down, you know...

GLYN What, Thackers?

STEPHANIE Yes, I heard that too somewhere... Fancy. Established nineteen twenty-seven.

GERRY *(gloomily)* Sign of the times. Sign of the times.

GLYN By the way – do you think she liked the clock I gave her? Mother?

GERRY She loved it. Did you not see her face when she opened it?

GLYN Yes I did. I thought she seemed a bit – disapproving.

GERRY She was over the moon with it.

GLYN I can take it back and change it.

STEPHANIE Don't bother. You did your best. You spent days choosing it. You never take that much trouble with my birthday.

GLYN Well, you – generally know what you want, don't you...?

Pause.

BENGIE *returns with a mop and bucket and hurries through.*

GERRY She's attractive, though. That girl. Good looker...

GLYN Oh, yes...

STEPHANIE Yes. *(She makes to rise)* Well, we must be thinking of—

GERRY Baby-sitters?

GLYN Yes, right—

STEPHANIE Otherwise we'll have to pay her for another two hours or something...

GLYN Probably tucked up in our bed with her boyfriend by now...

STEPHANIE *(grimly)* She'd better not be...

GERRY You bring the car?

GLYN Oh, yes...

GERRY You all right to drive?

STEPHANIE Who do you think's driving? Muggins here.

GERRY You're all right?

STEPHANIE Of course.

GERRY Only they've been tightening up...

STEPHANIE I've had half a glass all evening. You know I never do...

GLYN You hardly ate anything either...

STEPHANIE What do you mean? I ate mountains.

GLYN I was watching. Three mouthfuls and you pushed it away.

STEPHANIE Well, I ate a lot for me... Anyway, I have to be careful. I start putting on weight, you're the first to complain.

GLYN Never.

STEPHANIE You do. A tub of lard in tights, he called me the other night...

GLYN I did not, you called yourself that...

STEPHANIE Well, maybe I did but I didn't want you going repeating it in the pub, did I? In front of everyone?

GERRY You look lovely, Steph, you look a picture. *(He embraces* **STEPHANIE** *with mock passion)*

STEPHANIE Here's someone who appreciates me. *(She kisses* **GERRY***)* That was a lovely meal, thank you, Gerry... As always.

GERRY Well, it did cross my mind to take her somewhere else and then I thought, well... It's a tradition this place, isn't it? Every birthday, anniversary – we always seem to end up here. And it's your mother's favourite, so why not?

GLYN We've been using it a bit lately. From the office. It's quite convenient. Have you ever tried lunch here?

GERRY No, never lunch...

GLYN Very good. Reasonable prices, too, aren't they?

STEPHANIE Don't ask me. You never take me out to lunch.

GLYN I would do, I would do. You've only to ask...

GERRY I'd take him up on that, Steph.

STEPHANIE I will, don't worry.

GERRY I'll see you to the door...

STEPHANIE There's no need.

GERRY No, I'll get the bill at the same time— *(He stops them)* Listen, just before we... Steph. Glyn.

GLYN Yes.

GERRY I hope you appreciate, this business with you two getting together again – patching it up between you – it couldn't have been a better birthday present for her, I'm telling you.

STEPHANIE *(not wishing to prolong this)* Well, maybe—

GERRY No, Steph, I don't think you properly – I mean Glyn and I, we know her – and sometimes she comes over, you know, as maybe a bit blunt, plain spoken, you know. Even tough, sometimes, yes. Well, yes, Laura can be tough. But underneath all that, she's a very vulnerable woman. A very caring person and someone who gets hurt quite easily.

STEPHANIE Yes, I'm sure.

GERRY Now you two, you've had your moments – you and her, Steph. I know you have. You've had your disagreements but let's say, starting today, it's a new leaf, all right? A new leaf for you and her, Steph. And a new leaf for you two. Right.

GLYN Dead right.

GERRY *puts his arm around* **STEPHANIE**. **STEPHANIE** *stands rather awkwardly.*

GERRY You see, if anything happened to... Well, you know how we both care for Timmy, don't you?

STEPHANIE Oh, yes.

GERRY Laura's always – I think she's always secretly dreamt of grandchildren – I think she wanted grandchildren more than she wanted children...

STEPHANIE Difficult—

GLYN Oh, yes, she's always wanted them, I think... I mean she's never said it in so many words, but—

STEPHANIE Well, she's got one...

GERRY Yes, but when we thought, you know, you and Glyn were all washed up, I mean... Maybe not get to see Stephanie – and Timmy again...

STEPHANIE *(slightly impatiently)* Yes, we're back together now though, aren't we?

GERRY *(kissing her again)* Yes, you are! You are! *(To* **GLYN***)* And he's going to behave himself from now on, aren't you?

GLYN It's all in the past, Dad.

GERRY Send her packing. Do you hear?

GLYN I've sent her packing.

GERRY We used to have a word for women like that—

GLYN Yes, OK—

GERRY Not a very pleasant word—

STEPHANIE Sorry, Gerry, we really must go—

GERRY *(ignoring her)* No more, do you hear? No more.

GLYN No more, promise.

GERRY Word of honour?

GLYN Word of honour, Dad.

GERRY *(grasping* STEPHANIE *again)* You stand by this one, you hear me? You stand by this lovely girl or you'll have me to answer to next time—

ADAM *returns rather anxiously.*

STEPHANIE How is she?

ADAM She's all right, she's—

GLYN Does she need a lift anywhere...?

ADAM No, she's fine. I'll see her home. She just needs her handbag...

STEPHANIE Has she been sick?

ADAM Yes.

STEPHANIE Best thing.

ADAM In the Gents.

GERRY The Gents?

ADAM Yes.

GERRY Bloody hell, Adam.

ADAM She was in that much of a hurry she misread the signs...

GERRY There's a bright pink door and a bright blue door, what else does she need?

ADAM Well, she wasn't feeling too good...

GERRY All the women in the world and you have to take up with a colourblind hairdresser. I don't know... Is she still in there?

ADAM No, she's in the Ladies now...

GERRY Just as well. I want to use the other one...

ADAM I'll just get her bag. Take her home.

GERRY *(as he goes)* Bloody hell, I don't know. It's your mother's birthday, son.

> **GERRY** *goes out.*

ADAM Sorry.

STEPHANIE Take her home. She'll be all right. Probably have a bit of a hangover, that's all.

ADAM I don't know why she... She doesn't drink, you see. Normally. Hardly at all.

STEPHANIE I was saying, she was probably nervous.

ADAM Yes, she was. I mean, I told her there was no need to be but—

GLYN Nevermind. You know what they say about buses. There'll be another along in a minute. Same with women—

STEPHANIE Oh shut up, that's fat lot of help, isn't it...?

GLYN Plenty more fish—

ADAM It's not as simple as that. The trouble is – I'm in love with her—

GLYN *(laughing)* Oh, great...

ADAM I am.

GLYN Has there ever been one you haven't been in love with?

ADAM Not like this. Never like this.

STEPHANIE She's certainly in love with you...

ADAM You think so? How do you know?

STEPHANIE Because I was looking at her—

ADAM You could tell by looking at her?

STEPHANIE Of course. It was obvious. She couldn't take her eyes off you.

GLYN What do you mean? She was touching me up under the table for half the meal.

ADAM She was not!

STEPHANIE She certainly wasn't. Or I'd have cut her fingers off.

ADAM You really think she loves me?

STEPHANIE I keep saying. Hasn't she told you?

ADAM Yes, but...

STEPHANIE Then she most probably means it. *(Pleasantly to* GLYN*)* Some people do...

LAURA *returns.*

LAURA *(with some satisfaction)* Well, she looks a right mess now, I must say. I doubt if they'll let her in here again in a hurry.

ADAM I must take her bag to her. Is she all right?

LAURA As far as I know. I left her in there, washing her face. *(To* GLYN *and* STEPHANIE*)* She was sick in the Gents, you know. Not even the Ladies.

STEPHANIE Yes, we heard.

ADAM *starts to hunt for* MAUREEN's *handbag.*

LAURA There's a great queue of men waiting to get in while they clean up.

STEPHANIE Oh, dear.

LAURA Including your father.

STEPHANIE Oh, well. Good-night, Laura.

LAURA Oh, are you both off? Good-night, then.

LAURA *and* STEPHANIE *kiss quite sedately.*

And thank you for the lovely present, Steph. As I say, I'll wear them all the time. Good-night, Glyn. And thank you for the clock...

GLYN *(anxiously)* It was what you wanted, was it? You really liked it?

ADAM *(having located the bag under the table)* Excuse me...

LAURA Just a minute, Adam...

ADAM I just have to—

LAURA Just a quick word. *(She embraces* **GLYN**, *rather peremptorily)* Goodnight, dear.

GLYN 'Night, Mum. See you Thursday.

LAURA Thursday?

GLYN We're bringing Timmy up to visit you, aren't we?

LAURA *(unenthusiastically)* Oh yes, lovely.

STEPHANIE Good-night, Adam. And remember what I told you.

ADAM Oh, yes. Right. 'Night.

GLYN 'Night, Ad. *(As they go, to an unseen waiter)* Thank you. That was lovely.

STEPHANIE *(likewise)* Yes, lovely, yes. Thank you.

    STEPHANIE *and* **GLYN** *exit.*

LAURA What's she been telling you, then?

ADAM Who?

LAURA Stephanie. What was it she told you?

ADAM *(evasively)* Oh, nothing. I forget.

LAURA Well. I think you know what I'm going to say, don't you?

ADAM Yes.

LAURA Do I need to say it?

ADAM No. You don't like her. She's not right for me. She's common. She ate her melon with the wrong knife, I don't know—

LAURA Now, come on, be sensible—

ADAM She wears her shoes on the wrong feet—

LAURA Now I'm not like that, you know that. I'm not. You know you're free to choose. You're perfectly free. You're twenty-four years old in October and you're old enough by now to make your own mistakes.

ADAM Then I will.

LAURA All I'm saying is, we both care for you. You know that. We care for you more than anything in the world. So you have to see we both can't just stand by and say nothing at all. What sort of people would we be if we did that?

ADAM Yes, I realize that what you're saying you feel is for the—

LAURA If we stood there watching you throw your life away?

ADAM I'm not throwing my life away—

LAURA Adam, she's an alcoholic—

ADAM She's not an alcoholic—

LAURA Adam, darling, I've seen alcoholics. I've lived with them. Your own father's brother, your Uncle David, he was an alcoholic. Please don't try to teach me about alcoholics, Adam. Please. I'm telling you, that girl is a virtual alcoholic.

ADAM Mum, it was only tonight. She was nervous. She never drinks normally.

LAURA No, Adam, listen. Listen to what you're saying. What you're saying is, you've never normally caught her drinking...

ADAM I'd know if she drank. I'd know.

LAURA How could you know? How? You're not trained—

ADAM Well, I'm close to her. I kiss her and – things...

LAURA Oh, don't worry. There's ways. They have ways. Your Uncle David used to suck mothballs. Just to cover the smell...

ADAM No wonder he died.

LAURA He died of drink, Adam. Drink. With a liver the size of Wembley Stadium. After we'd all nursed him for two years. Watching him die. You want to finish up doing that?

ADAM Oh come on, this is ridiculous. Maureen's not—

LAURA Maureen's a young woman with a serious personal problem and a shrewd eye for the main chance—

ADAM I'm not listening to this—

LAURA Adam—

ADAM I'm not. I'm sorry.

LAURA Adam, do you want to break your father's heart? Because that's what you're going to end up doing—

ADAM Oh, bollocks—

LAURA You want to kill your own father, go ahead—

ADAM Oh, bugger off.

ADAM *storms off, passing* TUTO, *who enters.*

TUTO Good-night, seerar. Everything satisfactory? Good. We try to please. Madama Stratton, some more coffee?

LAURA (*tight-lipped*) Yes, I think I need some, Tuto. Thank you very much.

TUTO Cer-tainly! (*He makes to go*)

LAURA And I'll have a large Rémy Martin as well, please.

TUTO Large Rémy – cer-tainly.

TUTO *goes off cheerfully.*

LAURA *sits down again.*

GERRY *returns.*

GERRY Right then. I've asked for the bill.

LAURA He just swore at me.

GERRY Who did? The waiter?

LAURA No. Adam. He's just sworn at me. Told me to B-U-G off.

GERRY *(shrugging)* Well...

LAURA No, *not* "well". He shouldn't use language like that. Not to his mother. That's not how we brought him up. You'd have walloped him at one time.

GERRY I never walloped him, you wouldn't let me. It was Glyn I walloped...

LAURA Fat lot of good that did...

GERRY Anyway. He's upset. She's embarrassed him. He's upset. He's made a mistake. He realizes that.

LAURA Well, I only hope he does... He seems very stuck on her.

GERRY He's only got to take one look at her now. Enough to put him off for life. By God she looks a mess. All down her—

LAURA Yes, I know...

GERRY All over her dress and shoes. All down her tights.

LAURA Yes, I know, I saw her. You don't have to go into details—

GERRY Dear, oh dear. Ruined her dress.

LAURA I've no sympathy.

> **BENGIE** *enters with the brandy.*

Thank you.

GERRY What's that you're having?

LAURA A brandy.

GERRY Another one?

LAURA I needed it.

GERRY Well, in that case I'll join you... *(To* BENGIE*)* Oy! I say!
I say! I'll have a brandy as well—

BENGIE *shakes his head, not comprehending.*

A brandy. One brandy.

LAURA He doesn't speak English. Why can't they find waiters
that speak English?

GERRY Bran-deee. *(To* LAURA*)* They're all relations of Calvinu's.
He has them shipped over in packing cases.

BENGIE *(recognizing a word)* Calvinu! Mente! *("One moment")*

BENGIE *hurries out.*

GERRY Get some nice presents, did you?

LAURA Well, apart from yours, which is lovely, thank you very
much – I got some ear-rings from Stephanie, which I must
say for once I might actually wear occasionally. I've got
drawers full of stuff she's given me, I never touch. You'd
think she'd have noticed by now. Never known a woman
with so many friends that make cheap jewellery. That or
homemade pottery. Glyn? Glyn gave me that damn great
clock I certainly don't want and I've no idea where to put.
Adam gave me a lovely little book of poetry which he wrote
in, which was nice. He knows I like poetry. Well, some
poetry. As for that girl, I can't work out what she's given
me at all. A piece of knotted string as far as I can see. *(She
holds up the object in question)*

GLYN *(considering it)* Well...

LAURA I mean, what is it? You tell me...

GERRY Hang on, I know. It's one of those hanging things. For
hanging things in. Pots.

LAURA Pots?

GERRY For flowers. Flower pots. Hanging baskets. Probably
made it herself.

LAURA *(tossing the item aside)* Yes, I should think she probably did from the look of it.

TUTO *returns with a pot of coffee.*

TUTO More coffee? Delicious coffee.

LAURA Thank you.

TUTO Bengie bring you the brandy?

LAURA Yes. We want another one, please.

TUTO One more brandy. Rémy Martin, yes?

GERRY That'll do.

TUTO Seerar, more coffee?

GERRY Thank you.

TUTO *(calling off)* Hey, Bengie, ennesta gapay Rémy Martin. *("Another glass of Rémy Martin")* Rémy Martin! *(He shakes his head)* Yey yey yey. He's very young.

LAURA Yes?

TUTO He's also a little stupid.

GERRY Oh yes?

TUTO Very, very stupid. Otherwise why does he come over here, eh?

TUTO *goes off laughing.*

GERRY *and* LAURA *look slightly dubious.*

GERRY Well, at least they're back together. Glyn and Steph. That's the main thing.

LAURA How long for though...?

GERRY Oh, I think they'll make a go of it, this time. He's had his fling—

LAURA I know Glyn was largely to blame – I'm sure he'd drive any woman up the wall – but frankly I do think you'd have to be some sort of a saint to live with that girl for any length of time...

GERRY Stephanie?

LAURA I mean, she's not an easy person.

GERRY Oh, I get on with her. I like her.

LAURA You would, you're a man. She makes the effort for you. But I've seen her on her own. And I'll tell you this, underneath she is self-centred and selfish.

GERRY I won't hear a word against her—

LAURA I tell you she leads Glyn a dance. It's not all one way.

GERRY How do you mean? You mean she's having an affair?

LAURA No, I'm not saying that. She wouldn't have the nous. But you don't have to climb into bed with people to lead them a dance, do you?

GERRY I don't know what you're talking about.

LAURA You wouldn't, you're a man.

BENGIE *returns with a brandy.*

BENGIE Rémy Martin?

GERRY Yes, over here. Thank you.

BENGIE Rémy Martin.

GERRY Thank you.

BENGIE Rémy Martin. Thank you.

BENGIE *goes out.*

GERRY Cheers.

LAURA Good health.

They drink.

What'll happen to Adam, do you think? What'll become of him?

GERRY No idea, he's like you. I've never understood him, either.

LAURA He is. He's exactly like me. He's a worrier. That's what worries me. He ought to be settled. He ought to have found himself a career by now. A proper career. A proper woman.

GERRY Well, haven't I offered him a job with us? A decent job. Not a sinecure, maybe, but a safe job with the firm. Like Glyn has. Not Glyn's responsibilities, perhaps, but then Glyn's that bit more responsible, but still a responsible job, challenging.

LAURA He's destined for better things than that...

GERRY *(indignantly)* What do you mean, better things?

LAURA Just sitting behind a desk all day. That may be all right for Glyn—

GERRY He doesn't just sit behind a desk all day, what do you think we do...?

LAURA but then Glyn's got the imagination of a coat-hanger...

GERRY The job I offered Adam had good money, good prospects. Not a desk job either. Not at all. Using his brain, getting out and about. Meeting different people. There's a lot would be glad of that. But he'd rather waste his time with his poetry magazines and what have you...

LAURA That's not wasting time...

GERRY He's got a genius for timing, that boy. Four hundred businesses going to the wall every week, three million unemployed, world recession, God knows what else and he decides to start a bloody poetry magazine. I mean, he's a nice enough lad and he's your son but in my opinion he's a couple of sandwiches short of a picnic, that one.

LAURA *Our* son. He's *our* son. And it's an arts magazine. It covers all the arts. Locally.

GERRY *(uninterested)* Does it? Single sheet, is it?

LAURA He left you a copy only you never even looked at it.

GERRY I mean, we're feeling the pinch badly enough. And we're at the top end of the market, we are.

LAURA *(suddenly alert)* We're not in trouble, are we?

GERRY No. Not yet. If things go on as they are much longer we might be. But not yet.

LAURA My God. I'd no idea. You never talk to me about these things...

GERRY There's no point, is there? You're not interested.

LAURA I'm certainly interested if we're going broke—

GERRY We're not going broke—

LAURA You just said—

GERRY Keep your voice down. I said we might be if. That's all. If. Things go on as they are. That's all I said. But they probably won't do, so forget I said it. Forget all about it. Shut up about it, altogether. It's your birthday, for God's sake.

Pause.

LAURA I never realized we were in trouble...

The lights dim slightly on GERRY *and* LAURA, *who continue to sit silently sipping their brandies, both lost in their own thoughts. They will continue in "present" time. That is to say, the rest of the play, as far as they are concerned, is the remainder of their evening together – approximately two hours. For the other characters, time behaves somewhat differently. For* STEPHANIE *and* GLYN, *who are shortly to enter, theirs is "future" time which will stretch ahead over a period of two years. The lights crossfade to the downstage right corner table. It is lunchtime on Friday, 24th January, almost a week after* LAURA's *birthday dinner. It is raining hard outside.*

A waiter, **DINKA***, a rather sour man in his thirties, enters, leading* **STEPHANIE** *to the table. Despite the rain she has obviously made some effort with her appearance this morning.*

DINKA *(without ceremony)* Here, this one here.

STEPHANIE *(rather breathless from running)* Thank you.

DINKA It's all we got.

STEPHANIE It's fine. Can I get rid of my –? *(She indicates her wet coat)*

DINKA *holds out his hand without offering to help.*

(she struggles out of her coat) Terrible downpour. Just got caught in it. Of course I had to park miles away...you know... *(She hands* **DINKA** *her coat)* Thank you.

DINKA It's for one?

STEPHANIE No, I said there's two of us, my husband should be here any – *(She sees him)* Oh yes, there he is. *(She calls)* Glyn! *(To* **DINKA***)* Don't go away, he may want to order a drink.

DINKA You want a drink?

STEPHANIE No, I don't want one. My husband might want a drink. I'll just have some water, please.

DINKA You want water?

STEPHANIE Yes, some still water. Not fizzy—

GLYN *enters. Unlike* **STEPHANIE***'s, his clothes are hardly wet at all.*

GLYN Sorry... One drop of rain, every bit of traffic grinds to a halt.

STEPHANIE You didn't drive here...?

GLYN I wasn't getting drowned.

STEPHANIE You're only just round the corner. It's a two-minute walk.

GLYN I'm not walking, not in this.

STEPHANIE Did you get parked?

GLYN Yes, just outside.

STEPHANIE God, some people. I'm way over in Pond Street.

DINKA You want a drink?

GLYN Yes, I'll have a scotch with water. You want something?

DINKA Scotch with water.

GLYN You having something?

STEPHANIE Yes, just water.

DINKA Fizzy water?

STEPHANIE No, plain water, please.

DINKA *(moving away)* Plain water.

GLYN *(after* DINKA*)* And we'll have some menus at the same time. We're in a hurry.

DINKA Menus.

   DINKA *exits.*

GLYN I see we've got Cheerful Charlie.

STEPHANIE Is it usually this busy in here at lunchtimes?

GLYN Generally. So. How is she?

STEPHANIE Well, I was there for about an hour with her. And she was sitting up the whole time. She's still on drugs, of course, but she seems much brighter than she was. You know, talking and answering. Following what you're saying.

GLYN How's the bruising? Has that gone down?

STEPHANIE Yes. Well, it's still there of course – but her face is nearly back to normal. She doesn't look anything like as bad as she did.

GLYN How is she in herself...?

STEPHANIE Well, all right. As well as you can expect – it's going to take some time, Glyn... They were very close, weren't they?

GLYN They were. Inseparable.

STEPHANIE I don't think she's properly taken it in, really.

GLYN Did she mention him...? Did she ask about Dad?

STEPHANIE No. Not at all. Not once.

GLYN At least she's sitting up and taking notice.

STEPHANIE Yes, she is. Well, as much notice as she ever takes of me, which isn't a lot. She never enjoys talking to me. She wanted you there really. Or Adam, of course, ideally...

GLYN *(anxiously)* I hope you explained I was – I mean, I'll be up there first thing this evening—

STEPHANIE I told her you were busy—

GLYN You bet I was busy. But I can be there from this evening. All night, if necessary—

STEPHANIE You won't need to do that. She's being nursed. She's sedated. She'll be sleeping, anyway. Listen, how are things? At work?

GLYN Chaos. The trouble with Dad was, he wouldn't delegate. When he died, half the secrets died with him. Where the hell's Adam, then? Why hasn't he been up to see her? He hasn't got anything else to do.

STEPHANIE They said he looked in yesterday morning. He was there about ten minutes and fainted.

GLYN Fainted?

STEPHANIE Apparently.

GLYN What was the matter with him?

STEPHANIE Nothing. Just hospitals, I think.

GLYN Typical.

STEPHANIE He brought that Maureen along with him. That didn't help. You know how your mother feels about Maureen.

GLYN What did she do this time, throw up all over the bed?

STEPHANIE No, she's not like that, not at all. She's a nice kid. She brought your mother some paper flowers.

GLYN Paper flowers?

STEPHANIE Yes, she'd made them herself. Out of tissue paper. They were beautiful. She's ever so clever with her hands.

GLYN Did Mother appreciate them?

STEPHANIE Oh, you know her, she chucked them in the bin soon as they'd left. I picked them out, though, and brought them home—

GLYN *(looking around, impatiently)* Where's this man gone to? I want to order.

STEPHANIE they look lovely in that alcove above the telly.

GLYN I've got meeting after meeting this afternoon. You've no idea.

STEPHANIE Will you be home late again?

GLYN Probably. I'll pop up and see Mother, of course. I may have to come back. Sorry.

STEPHANIE No. Thanks for finding time for lunch. Haven't seen you for days, have I?

GLYN Won't last for ever. Back to normal soon.

STEPHANIE I hope so. I miss you. So does Timmy.

GLYN I miss you.

STEPHANIE Do you? Really?

GLYN Of course.

STEPHANIE You really miss us? You're not just saying that?

GLYN Of course not. I wouldn't say it if I didn't mean it, would I?

STEPHANIE You might.

GLYN Why should I? Why should I do that?

STEPHANIE Well – to keep me quiet.

GLYN You think I'd do that?

STEPHANIE You have done in the past, haven't you? Said you loved me when you were—

GLYN Now, that's in the past. Well in the past. All right? That's forgotten. We agreed. All right?

STEPHANIE Yes.

GLYN I gave you my word, didn't I?

STEPHANIE Yes.

GLYN I promised you. And I promised...

STEPHANIE You promised who?

GLYN I promised Mum and Dad.

STEPHANIE You promised them?

GLYN Yes.

STEPHANIE When? When did you do that?

GLYN Oh, last Saturday evening, when we were all together... on her birthday, you know.

STEPHANIE Why?

GLYN Why what?

STEPHANIE Why did you promise them? What's it to do with them?

GLYN It's everything to do with them. I'm their son for one thing.

STEPHANIE It's our marriage...

GLYN Yes, and they – they were anxious that it succeeded.

STEPHANIE Why?

GLYN Because they wanted us to be happy. That's natural, isn't it?

STEPHANIE But we weren't happy, were we?

GLYN No, maybe we weren't then. But we are now, aren't we?

STEPHANIE Yes, we are now. But they weren't to know we would be, were they? When you left me and went off to live with *her* that was because you were no longer happy with me, wasn't it? You were happier with *her*, weren't you? So if they'd had your happiness at heart they'd have suggested you stayed with *her*, wouldn't they? Instead of coming back to me?

GLYN I came back to you because I wanted to come back to you... Me. I decided it. Nobody else. Me. All right?

STEPHANIE Then why did you need to make promises to them?

GLYN Just to keep them happy, that's all...

STEPHANIE I see. Did you promise her anything? Just to keep *her* happy?

GLYN No, I did not. Don't be stupid.

STEPHANIE I just wondered.

GLYN She's got a name you know. *Her*. She's got a name.

STEPHANIE I prefer *her*.

GLYN Fair enough.

Slight pause.

STEPHANIE We are happy, aren't we?

GLYN Yes. We're happy. I think we're happy. Aren't we? Pretty happy, anyway. Who the hell ever knows when they're happy? I don't know.

*At this point, the owner of the restaurant, **ERNESTO CALVINU**, enters. He is an ample man in late middle age. He carries a tray on which is the whisky, a small jug of water, a bottle of carbonated water and an extra glass. Under his arm are two menus.*

Ah, Ernesto!

CALVINU Mr Stratton. What can I say? I am so, so sorry. I am devastated. We are all devastated. In the kitchen. All the waiters, the cashier, the hat check girl. Such a loss. Such a loss...

GLYN It is. It is.

CALVINU When we heard, we couldn't believe – the same Mr Stratton? My friend Gerry who was in here all these years? Unbelievable.

GLYN Yes, it is. Unbelievable.

CALVINU Unbelievable.

GLYN Darling, you know Ernesto, don't you – Ernesto Calvinu?

STEPHANIE Yes, of course, we've—

CALVINU Of course, of course. Only the other night. Madama, please excuse me. This news has made me – all over the place—

STEPHANIE Of course.

CALVINU Gerry Stratton and I. We were old friends. Only the other night you were all here. Your poor mother... Poor Laura.

GLYN Yes—

CALVINU It was the same night? The car?

GLYN Yes. He was driving home from here with my mother—

CALVINU Your mother—

GLYN and they – just came off the road—

CALVINU off the road—

GLYN no other vehicle—

CALVINU no vehicle, no—

GLYN and - it's a mystery.

CALVINU It's a mystery. It's a mystery. It's a mystery.

GLYN Yes.

CALVINU Mystery, hmm?

GLYN Yes.

CALVINU But your mother? She's all right?

GLYN She's—

STEPHANIE She'll be fine.

CALVINU Excuse me. Your drinks. Scotch and water.

GLYN Thank you.

CALVINU Fizzy water for the lady.

STEPHANIE Oh, I really wanted—

CALVINU Please. On the house. On the house.

GLYN Thank you.

STEPHANIE Thank you.

CALVINU Please. The menus. Madama, Seerar.

STEPHANIE Thank you.

GLYN Thank you.

CALVINU The special today is vissviss. That is minced beef cooked very, very rare and served on red cabbage with a sauce of fresh beetroot. *(He looks at them)* Maybe not today, though? 'Scoos. I will leave you in peace.

GLYN Thank you.

STEPHANIE Thank you.

CALVINU *departs.*

A silence.

GLYN Nice man. Well, what are you going to have then?

The lights dim on the table downstage right and crossfade to the main table, centre. GERRY *and* LAURA *are seated as before, still sipping their brandy. It is, in their time scale, a few moments later.*

LAURA I mean, if we're going bankrupt I think I should be told about it, don't you?

GERRY *(irritably)* We're not going bankrupt. Who said we were going bankrupt?

LAURA That's what you seemed to be hinting at just now.

GERRY We're a long way from being bankrupt. A long way. We just have – one or two cash-flow problems, that's all. Actually, if you must know, they're not our problems at all. They're other people's problems. Only they get passed on. Their problem becomes your problem, that's all.

LAURA So there is a problem, then?

GERRY Yes, there's a problem. There's a problem. But it's solvable. They always are, problems. That's what they're put there for.

LAURA What do you do to solve it? I mean, if you're running out of money how do you solve it?

GERRY You use your imagination, don't you? Make creative use of what you've got.

LAURA Creative? What's creative?

GERRY You know, like that son of yours gets...

LAURA I presume you're referring to Adam?

GERRY He's the only creative one round here, isn't he? He's our poet.

LAURA He's not a poet.

GERRY Oh, I beg his pardon. I thought that's what he was this week.

LAURA He edits a magazine. If you read it, you'd know...

GERRY Pop video maker, entrepreneur – whatever that is – documentary film director – television cameraman – he was going to be one of them for a bit, wasn't he? And what happened to that theatre he was going to open? Haven't heard much about that lately either, have we?

LAURA Leave him alone. He doesn't bother you. He never asks you for money, does he?

GERRY No, he doesn't. He asks you and that's worse.

LAURA I can do what I like with my money.

GERRY And who gives you that money in the first place, may I ask?

LAURA You do.

GERRY Precisely.

LAURA And I earn every bloody penny of it, so don't you start that one.

  Pause.

GERRY *(suddenly bad tempered)* I want another brandy.

LAURA It's gone half-past eleven—

GERRY Who cares, I want another brandy. *(He calls)* Hey! Hey, waiter! *(He rises)* Oh, what the hell, I'll get it myself, it's quicker.

LAURA He'll be back in a minute, he's busy.

GERRY I need the Gents as well. Hopefully they'll have cleaned it up by now.

  He goes out.

LAURA *(after him)* Don't order anything for me, will you...

The lights fade on the main table and come up on the table downstage left. **ADAM** *and* **MAUREEN** *are seated at the table and have apparently just finished a meal together. Their time is "past" time. From their viewpoint we are now one week prior to the birthday supper, on an evening earlier that same month, Saturday, 11th January. We will follow them gradually further back in time over a period of two months to the point where they first met.* **MAUREEN** *is sitting miserably, playing with objects on the table, fidgety and uncertain.*

ADAM *(gently)* Come on, Mo, what is it? What's the matter?

MAUREEN *(in a small voice)* Nothing. I've said it's nothing.

ADAM Don't keep saying nothing. Something is. Something must be. Come on, what is it? Mo?

MAUREEN *shakes her head but refuses to answer.*

Well, I don't know. I don't know what I'm supposed to have said. What am I supposed to have said? Whatever it is I'm supposed to have said, I'm sorry I said it – if I said it.

MAUREEN You haven't said anything. It's not you. It's not your fault. It's everything.

ADAM What do you mean, everything?

MAUREEN It's—

AGGI, *another waiter, interrupts them.* **AGGI** *is middle-aged and has adopted the couple ever since they first started eating there together. Indeed, they first fell in love at one of his tables, so he feels responsible for their continuing happiness. He is given to sudden bursts of unaccompanied, full-blooded singing – folk songs in his native tongue – which he fondly hopes will further the course of true love.*

AGGI More coffees? Liqueurs? Brandies? Ports? No?

MAUREEN No.

ADAM No, thank you.

AGGI *(singing softly and with great feeling)*

> SO NISS PRO NENTOY,
> SAR BEEEEEE TARIN-TAIR.
> CHIN NEEEE BOOLENTOY,
> OH NON TEE BRUNTO...

He finishes, pausing dramatically.

So.

AGGI goes. The pair have barely registered his recital.

ADAM What do you mean, everything?

MAUREEN It's just your parents and—

ADAM My parents? What about my parents?

MAUREEN It's all become so – important, hasn't it?

ADAM How do you mean? You mean to you? Important to you?

MAUREEN No. To you.

ADAM Me? I don't care. I don't give a stuff.

MAUREEN You do give a stuff, that's the point. You give a huge stuff. I wish you didn't.

ADAM I don't. I do what I like. I always have done. I don't take any notice of them. I don't care what they think.

MAUREEN But you want them to like me, don't you?

ADAM I don't mind either way...

MAUREEN You need them to approve—

ADAM I really don't—

MAUREEN You do, Adam. You do, you know.

ADAM I don't know why you should think that.

MAUREEN Because you keep going on about it. "Maureen, when you meet them, don't say this, will you? Don't say that".

ADAM When did I –?

MAUREEN "Don't wear that, will you, they won't approve of that. Be careful not to swear, will you? Don't say condoms, pessaries and penis in front of my mother, will you?"

ADAM *(looking round, alarmed)* Sssh!

MAUREEN I've even dyed my bloody hair for her...

ADAM Oh come on...

MAUREEN It's true.

ADAM You didn't dye it for her...

MAUREEN Who else? Who else did I dye it this bloody boring colour for?

ADAM You.

MAUREEN Me. Why should I do that? I hate it like this. I loathe it. I detest it like this. I can't bear to look at myself...

ADAM Well. For me then.

MAUREEN Do you like it like this?

ADAM Well, I...yes...

MAUREEN Better than the way it was before?

ADAM Er – well...

MAUREEN Exactly. It's for her. I dyed it for your mother. So I'd look dead ordinary. I haven't even met the woman and I've dyed my hair for her.

ADAM You didn't need to.

MAUREEN I did need to.

ADAM Why?

MAUREEN Because.

ADAM Yes?

MAUREEN Because. I want to be right for you. I want to look right for you. Because it matters so much to you – no, don't argue, it does – and it has to be right. You need their approval so I have to be right for you.

ADAM You are right for me.

MAUREEN I hope so. I really, really hope I am. I've got all my hopes on you, Adam.

ADAM So what if they don't approve? What the hell? What's it matter? We'll have to spend next Christmas on our own, won't we? Won't make a scrap of difference to me, the way I feel about you. Just be you, that's all. Be yourself. That's who I fell in love with. That's who I love. Don't you see?

MAUREEN I hope you believe that.

ADAM I do. *(Slight pause)* Well.

MAUREEN And you think that blue dress I bought will be all right? For this party?

ADAM It's not a party, I've said. It's just dinner, that's all. Supper. Us six for supper. Here in this restaurant. Quite informal. Nothing flash...

MAUREEN You think that dress is too much, then?

ADAM It's perfect. Come as you like, they're not fussy. My father never dresses up these days if he can help it. He'll probably come in an old sweater, knowing him...

MAUREEN What about your mother?

ADAM Well, my mother – yes, she'll probably wear something a bit—

MAUREEN And what about whatsername, your brother's wife?

ADAM Steph? Well...she's usually fairly casual. She'll probably wear a dress of some sort—

MAUREEN Short or long?

ADAM I don't know. Short.

MAUREEN How short?

ADAM Well, you know, long short, I don't know. Come in your jeans, what does it matter?

Slight pause.

MAUREEN I hope it's not too boring...

ADAM What, the party?

MAUREEN No, that dress I bought. I don't usually wear things like that. I could maybe put a bit of bright jewellery with it, just to cheer it up.

ADAM *(slightly anxious)* Not too much.

MAUREEN No. Do you think those ear-rings I wore the other night would do? You know. The parakeets?

ADAM Oh, yes. The big ones, you mean?

MAUREEN Yes. Do you think they'd go with it?

ADAM *(uncertainly)* Yes.

MAUREEN No?

ADAM Have you got any others?

MAUREEN I'll wear the studs.

ADAM Wear the parakeets if you like.

MAUREEN No, they're wrong. They're definitely wrong. I'll wear my opal studs.

ADAM They're nice.

MAUREEN You gave them to me. *(Remembering)* Oh, yes, look. Before I forget. *(She rummages under the table for her bag)* You must tell me – don't be afraid to tell me if this is wrong. If it's wrong I won't be offended. But you must tell me if it's the sort of thing she likes. *(She produces the string plant holder that she will later give to* LAURA. *She holds up the gift)* What do you think?

ADAM Yes. Yes. *(He studies it)* What is it exactly?

MAUREEN It's macramé. It's for holding a plant holder. You put it in here. Then you hang it up. Like that. Do you see?

ADAM Oh yes, that's great.

MAUREEN Is it the sort of thing she likes, do you think?

ADAM Oh, yes. She'll love it.

MAUREEN Really?

ADAM Oh, yes.

MAUREEN I made it myself.

ADAM Yes.

MAUREEN I couldn't think what to buy her that wasn't either terribly expensive – and then I thought—

ADAM You don't have to give her anything, you know. You haven't even met her.

MAUREEN Oh, I have to give her something if I'm going to her party.

ADAM It's just supper. There's the book. The poetry book I got her. That could be from both of us, if you want.

MAUREEN No, I'd like to give her something personal. From me. I think that's important. So long as you think this is right?

ADAM It's great.

MAUREEN Took me hours.

ADAM Yes.

MAUREEN I kept going wrong. I haven't made one since I was at school. Used to make masses of them at school. All we ever did at school, actually.

ADAM *(taking her hands)* It'll be a great evening, you wait and see? Trust me. They'll love you. And you'll love them.

MAUREEN Yes. You're right. It s going to be *great*, isn't it? And if they don't like me – well, fuck 'em.

They smile at each other.

ADAM You – er...you won't use language like that in front of them, will you?

As a frown of uncertainty returns to **MAUREEN***'s face, the lights fade on them. There is a crossfade to the main table where* **LAURA** *is seated as before. It's a few minutes later.*

GERRY *returns immediately. He carries two glasses of brandy.*

GERRY Here you are.

LAURA I said, I didn't want one.

GERRY You've got it.

LAURA Remember, you're driving.

GERRY So I am. *(He sits)* Just been talking to old Ernesto.

LAURA Oh, yes.

GERRY He's had a big party on upstairs. They've nearly finished. Said he'd pop down and have a word.

LAURA We're not going to be too late, are we?

GERRY Come on. Don't be so bloody miserable. It's your birthday.

LAURA Only for another twenty minutes, it is. *(Pause)* What was she wearing? What did she think she was wearing?

GERRY Who?

LAURA That girl of Adam's.

GERRY A dress, wasn't it?

LAURA She must have thought she was going to an embassy cocktail party...

GERRY Showed off a lot of her... Very nice.

LAURA Thoroughly common. Common as dirt.

GERRY Oh, I don't think so. Apparently her father breeds race horses.

LAURA Does he?

GERRY So she informed me.

LAURA *(digesting this)* Well...

GERRY And her mother's a french horn player with the Hallé Orchestra.

LAURA I find that hard to swallow, I must say.

GERRY Why should she lie about it?

LAURA What? All of them living in that little back-to-back on the side of the canal in Harwick Road?

GERRY *(shrugging)* Well...

LAURA God, I feel depressed. Why do I feel so depressed?

GERRY Because you're fifty-four today, my love.

LAURA That'll do it, dear. Thanks a bunch.

Another gloomy silence descends on both of them as the lights cross-fade to STEPHANIE, *at the table downstage right. She is finishing a grapefruit cocktail in a solitary state. She has evidently spent a great deal of time and trouble with her appearance. It is now almost a month later for her; a lunchtime on Friday, 14th February.*

TUTO, *full of the joys of spring as ever, bounces over to her.*

TUTO Madama, you enjoy that?

STEPHANIE Yes, it was lovely. Thank you.

TUTO Can't eat it all, no?

STEPHANIE A bit too much, that's all.

TUTO You want to go on? You want to wait for him?

STEPHANIE Er – I don't know, really. I can't think where he's got to.

TUTO Come on, you go on. You don't wait for him. It's Valentine's Day. What sort of husband stand up his beautiful wife on Valentine's Day? He don't deserve you, eh?

STEPHANIE *smiles faintly.*

Tell you what, in half an hour I come off duty, I come and eat with you, be your valentine, how about that?

STEPHANIE I might take you up on that, be careful...

TUTO You want to order?

STEPHANIE No – I'll just have some water, please. Some still water.

TUTO Still water. Running deep. OK. Right away. *(He sees someone)* Hey look! About time too! What time does he call this, eh?

GLYN *enters, hurriedly.*

TUTO *hovers.*

GLYN Sorry, darling.

STEPHANIE Where have you been? I had to start—

GLYN *(kissing her, briefly)* I'm sorry. I promised you lunch and then—

STEPHANIE What kept you?

GLYN Trouble.

TUTO A drink for seerar?

STEPHANIE What trouble?

GLYN Tell you later. Large scotch with water and I'll order straight away.

TUTO Large scotch with water, right away. Seerar, the menu. Thank you.

TUTO *goes off.*

STEPHANIE What's the problem?

GLYN I've been with the auditors...

STEPHANIE And?

GLYN God knows what the old boy was playing at. Money missing from here. Money deposited there with no record at all of how it got there. Where it came from. I don't know how he got away with it. Anyway, God knows what we owe, what we're owed – what's in profit...what isn't. God knows.

STEPHANIE But surely he had to keep records? He couldn't just have—

GLYN Oh, there are plenty of records. And at first glance everything's fine. Couldn't be rosier. He'd just taken a number of what he obviously considered were – like, temporary financial emergency measures. He was dead crafty. He was a genius. He's like a man who puts a building up without bothering with walls. It all looks wonderful till somebody tries to stand on the roof.

STEPHANIE I can't believe he was crooked. Not Gerry.

GLYN He wasn't crooked. Not at all. Well, no more than most. Better than a lot, really. Only usually they get the chance to tidy things up before they quit. They don't get hurled off the inner ring road in their prime.

TUTO *returns with a large scotch and water and a bottle of carbonated water for* STEPHANIE.

TUTO One water with scotch. One fizzy water without scotch.

STEPHANIE *(feebly)* I did ask for – er...

TUTO Seerar, you want to order?

GLYN Yeah – do you want a starter?

STEPHANIE No. I've had mine. But you go ahead. You have yours...

GLYN No, we'll go straight to the main course, no problem...

STEPHANIE No, have a starter.

GLYN Then you'll have to sit and watch me...

STEPHANIE I don't mind.

GLYN No, we'll both have a main course.

STEPHANIE No, I don't want a main course...

GLYN You don't want a main course?

STEPHANIE No.

GLYN Why not?

STEPHANIE I just don't.

GLYN You don't mind if I have a main course?

STEPHANIE No, you have what you like. I say, I'll just have the water.

GLYN You don't want pudding, either?

STEPHANIE I don't want anything.

GLYN Then why the hell do you come out to lunch if you don't want to eat?

STEPHANIE Why the hell do you think?

GLYN I can't imagine.

STEPHANIE (angrily) To see you. How else do I get to see you? Book an appointment?

GLYN (calming down) OK. Here I am.

TUTO Seerar. You want to order?

GLYN Yes, I'll order.

TUTO You want the special Valentine's Day Meal? Very nice.

GLYN No, no. Do you have any crimpledoos?

TUTO Crimpledoos? Oh yes. Freshly made. Very delicious.

GLYN I'll have a plate of that.

TUTO Crimpledoos. Nothing for the lady?

GLYN Nothing for the lady, apparently.

> **TUTO** *departs.*

You'll slip through the floorboards at this rate if you don't eat.

STEPHANIE *(wryly)* Hardly.

GLYN You should eat.

STEPHANIE I do eat.

GLYN When? When do you eat?

STEPHANIE I eat when I feel like it.

GLYN I don't want you getting ill.

STEPHANIE I'm all right.

GLYN I've got enough on my plate without an anorexic wife.

> *Slight pause.*

Sorry. I seem to remember this was supposed to be a romantic little luncheon.

STEPHANIE Yes.

GLYN Yes. Sorry. *(He smiles at her)*

> *She smiles back.*

How was your morning? Better than mine, I hope?

STEPHANIE Some of it. I spent the first two hours on the phone to your mother.

GLYN How is she?

STEPHANIE Oh, she's perfectly all right. She's decided this week to sell the house and go and live in France, that's the latest.

GLYN France? I thought it was Italy?

STEPHANIE No, that was last week.

GLYN My mistake. Can't keep up with her.

Slight pause.

STEPHANIE Actually I'm...

GLYN Hmm?

STEPHANIE I've – er... I don't quite know how you're going to take this. I went to the doctor's this morning and—

GLYN What for—

STEPHANIE Well, it was just—

GLYN *(angrily)* You are ill, aren't you? I knew this would happen. I said it would happen. I've told you to look after yourself—

STEPHANIE It's all right—

GLYN haven't I told you again and again to eat properly –?

STEPHANIE it's all right—

GLYN all this bloody stupid slimming—

STEPHANIE *(shouting him down)* It's all right. I'm pregnant, that's all, I'm only pregnant, that's all!

Silence.

GLYN *(stunned)* Pregnant?

STEPHANIE Are you pleased? I hope you're pleased. I am. Well, I am if you are, let's put it that way.

GLYN I'm—

STEPHANIE You're angry, aren't you?

GLYN No, of course not, I'm—

STEPHANIE You're pleased? You're delighted? You're ecstatic? You couldn't give a toss either way?

GLYN No, I'm pleased, I'm pleased for you. Of course I am. *(He searches for something to say)* Congratulations.

STEPHANIE You had a hand in it, too. Well, maybe not a hand but—

GLYN When did we – when was it we...?

STEPHANIE I think it was the night of the party – Mother's birthday...

GLYN Oh, yes.

STEPHANIE It had to be. We were in a bit of a hurry...

GLYN *(smiling)* Yes. Bit drunk.

STEPHANIE Not that drunk, do you mind?

GLYN No, not that drunk.

They smile at each other.

STEPHANIE Congratulations to you.

GLYN Thank you. *(He is still taking in the news)* God!

STEPHANIE That's shut you up, hasn't it?

At this moment TUTO *arrives with a plateful of something that could be pasta.*

TUTO Crimpledoos.

GLYN Thank you.

TUTO Benzay appertass!

TUTO *goes off.*

GLYN *picks up a fork and proffers it to* STEPHANIE.

GLYN Listen, half of this is yours. OK?

STEPHANIE *(cheerfully)* Benzay appertass!

As they both sit and eat together, the lights fade on them and, simultaneously come up on ADAM *and* MAUREEN, *at the table downstage left. Her appearance has undergone a slight change. Indeed, as we progress further back, the real, original* MAUREEN *will slowly be revealed. A much less conventional girl, exotically clad in vivid colours and bold ornamentation. But much of this awaits us in the past. At this point, only her hair colour has changed, back to its original bright shade. They both wear paper hats, courtesy of the management, and are studying the sweet menus,* MAUREEN *rather listlessly.*

ADAM Well? What are you going to have then?

MAUREEN Nothing.

ADAM Nothing?

MAUREEN I'm not hungry.

ADAM Since when?

MAUREEN Since now.

ADAM Five minutes ago you were starving. Couldn't wait to get at the sweet trolley...

MAUREEN Well, I'm not anymore.

ADAM I'm having something.

MAUREEN Have it.

ADAM What's got into you all of a sudden?

MAUREEN Nothing.

ADAM This is meant to be our Christmas dinner, you know.

MAUREEN I know.

ADAM Come on. Happy Christmas, then.

MAUREEN It's not Christmas, though, is it?

ADAM Nearly.

MAUREEN It's December the twentieth. That's not Christmas. I want to spend Christmas with you. Not just December the twentieth.

ADAM Well, you can't. I've said. Not this year. I have to spend it with my family. I can't just—

MAUREEN All right. Spend it with them. But why can't I come as well?

ADAM Because. Ours is always a family Christmas. We don't invite outsiders. It's tradition. It's just family.

MAUREEN I bet that sister-in-law of yours – what's her name, your brother's wife—

ADAM Stephanie.

MAUREEN Stephanie. I bet that Stephanie will be there?

ADAM Of course she will. She's family.

MAUREEN Not really. She's not a blood relation.

ADAM She's married to Glyn. She's related by marriage...

MAUREEN Well, we're engaged. We're related by engagement.

ADAM It's not the same thing.

MAUREEN I bet when she was engaged to your brother, she came home with him for Christmas.

ADAM *(warily)* I can't remember.

MAUREEN She did, didn't she? I'm right.

ADAM It was a long time ago.

MAUREEN Then why can't I?

Pause.

Don't answer.

ADAM What about your family? Aren't you going home to them?

MAUREEN I will if you'll come with me.

ADAM I can't.

MAUREEN No, of course you can't. Anyway, I wouldn't subject
you to that. I hate them. I hate them all. I hate my sister,
she's foul – she's got horrible crinkly hair and pink wallpaper.
And she has this revolting bald husband who puts glass
doors in everywhere and a squealing baby with an orange
face that you really want to sit on. And my mother, she's vile,
she's so low, she's really low. She sits there smoking these
horrible home-made fags and coughing and complaining.
And me grandad's incontinent and the dog's always got
worms and the whole place stinks of stale bacon fat and I
wouldn't go back there if you paid me.

Pause.

ADAM I can't keep up with your family.

Pause.

Every time you tell me about them, they're different.

Pause.

So you won't be going home, then?

MAUREEN Probably. I always do in the end. Get pissed with
me grandad. It's all right, really. It soon passes, Christmas,
doesn't it? He's quite funny after three bottles. Anyway, I'll
have to. I can't come home with you because you're ashamed
of me and I'm not staying here on my own, no way.

ADAM I'm not ashamed of you...

MAUREEN No?

ADAM I love you.

MAUREEN I know you do. You're still ashamed of me, though—

AGGI *enters with the sweet trolley. He is singing a lyrical ballad, softly and with feeling, especially for them.*

AGGI *(singing)*

SELENTAY...
CORENTAY...
PASSALAY...
UNCHENTAY...

MAUREEN Hallo, he's back—

AGGI *(singing, as he presents them with the sweet trolley)*

ARRANTAY...
NOVILO...
DECANTO...
DEVINO...
(He speaks) Puddings. For the lovers...

MAUREEN No, thank you.

AGGI No? No love puddings for madametta...?

MAUREEN No, no love puddings, no thank you, Aggi. Not tonight.

AGGI *(resuming his song)*

HONTAY...
CONSENTAY...

ADAM I'll have – what's that one at the top? The chocolate one? I'll have a piece of that.

AGGI Chooker. Delicious. *(He sings as he serves it, a new tune)*

TELLY MAT
...LA MARRACHO
TENNA RASTU E LAY TO...
(He speaks) Some cream...?

ADAM Yes, loads of cream.

MAUREEN Uggghh!

ADAM You want a bit?

MAUREEN No, I don't. *(To* AGGI*)* Do you have any Christmas pudding?

AGGI Christmas pudding? No, we don't have Christmas pudding. Some shups? That is raspberry sponge cake with almonds?

MAUREEN No, I only want Christmas pudding. I won't have anything, in that case.

ADAM Have some wine, there's some wine left here.

MAUREEN I don't want it. I don't drink, you know that.

ADAM You do.

MAUREEN Half a glass. It's not worth it. It has no effect on me at all.

AGGI *(presenting the sweet with a flourish)* Seerar!

ADAM Thank you.

AGGI Some coffee to follow?

ADAM Maybe in a minute.

AGGI Then maybe in a minute, I will return. Enjoy! Benzay appertass!

Singing.

HOO TIE ROOOOO...
SHILL LEEES OH MAAAYYYY...

AGGI *goes off with the sweet trolley, singing.*

MAUREEN Do you suppose he sings at everybody like that?

ADAM I don't know.

MAUREEN Does he sing at your parents, when they come here?

ADAM I doubt it. I think it's just for us. It's quite romantic.

MAUREEN Yes, it is. Could get on your nerves after a bit though, couldn't it?

ADAM I'll ask him to stop—

MAUREEN No, he's enjoying himself.

ADAM I thought you liked it.

MAUREEN I do normally, it's just tonight...

ADAM *(anxiously)* Are you sorry we got engaged?

MAUREEN Of course not. I'm very excited we got engaged. It's the most wonderful thing that ever happened to me. It's the only wonderful thing that ever happened to me, as a matter of fact, getting engaged to you... I just wish we could...

ADAM What?

MAUREEN I wish we could tell somebody else about it.

ADAM We will.

MAUREEN When?

ADAM Soon, as soon as—

MAUREEN As soon as you've told your parents?

ADAM Yes.

MAUREEN And as soon as I've had their seal of approval, presumably. And when will that be –?

ADAM Well—

MAUREEN Oh, God. Don't bother. Give me a spoonful of that and shut up.

He offers her a spoonful.

I try, you know. Look, I've got my little finger stuck out and everything. *(She studies him as she eats from his spoon)* It's dead important to you, isn't it? That they approve of me? That they like me? Answer me. It is, isn't it?

ADAM Yes, I suppose it is.

A silence. ADAM looks very unhappy. MAUREEN absently spoons some more pudding off his plate.

I love you. I love you so much, you've no idea.

MAUREEN My God, sometimes parents have a lot to answer for, don't they? *(She swallows the spoonful of pudding)* Hey! This is *good!*

She grabs ADAM's *bowl and sets about the rest of the contents. He watches her; still not very happily. The lights fade on them and come up on* GERRY *and* LAURA *at the table, centre. A silence of several minutes has existed between them ever since we were last with them.*

GERRY Well... Depressed or not...the evening's not been completely wasted. At least we've got them back together...

LAURA *(in her own thoughts)* Mmm?

GERRY Glyn and Stephanie. And Timmy. At least they're settled.

LAURA Till the next time.

GERRY There'll be no next time.

LAURA You sound very certain.

GERRY He gave me his word.

LAURA He what?

GERRY Glyn. That he wouldn't do it again. He gave me his word.

LAURA Rubbish!

GERRY This evening. In the Gents.

LAURA How can he do that? How can anybody give his word on that? Certainly not Glyn. It's in his nature. First good-looking typist he meets in the lift, he'll have his trousers round his ankles soon as look at her...

GERRY He's not like that—

LAURA Mind you. Married to a dried-up prune of a girl like her, who'd blame him.

GERRY Oh, come on—

LAURA I'm certain she keeps him on short rations, I'm sure she does...

GERRY How can you know that?

LAURA You can tell. You can always tell. You can tell from a woman's appetites. She toys with her food, she sips at her wine, she picks at her men. *(As if to make her point, she drains the rest of her brandy glass in a single gulp)*

GERRY I've never heard any of this. It's all nonsense.

LAURA How do you know? You don't know a bloody thing about women. You never have done. You think we're from another planet. You're not interested in them. Take them or leave them, you. Mostly leave them.

GERRY How much have you had to drink?

LAURA Enough. *(Angrily)* It's my birthday, isn't it? What the hell's it to you?

GERRY All right. Come on, come on. Simmer down. What's the matter with you?

Pause.

(in an attempt to lighten things) Behave yourself, woman. I'll put you over my knee in a minute.

LAURA Yes, you've done that in your time, haven't you?

GERRY I have not, what are you talking about?

LAURA Oh yes, you've hit me before now...

GERRY Rubbish.

LAURA It's true.

GERRY Only – only when you drove me to it...

LAURA Only when you cared enough to bother, you mean.

GERRY *(muttering)* I don't know why we're dragging this up. It was years ago.

Pause.

LAURA No, in that respect – and only in that respect I hasten to add – Glyn's like me. He's inherited my needs. My appetites. We're not the sort to sit and pick at our food. Never have been.

GERRY What are you talking about? You're both the same as everybody else. We're all made exactly the same. We all want the same thing equally badly. Only some of us control it. Some of us don't. It's strength of mind, that's all it is. I can control it, I've never strayed. I won't say I've never been tempted but I've controlled it. Whereas Glyn obviously can't. Adam, well, I think he probably can, who the hell knows with him? You can, Stephanie can – so far as I know...

LAURA How do you know?

GERRY What?

LAURA You're saying this with great authority but how do you know...?

GERRY I think we can safely assume—

LAURA Well, I don't think you can. And frankly I don't think you should.

GERRY What is this? Do you know something about Stephanie that I don't know? Has she been carrying on as well?

LAURA Her? She'd never have the energy to climb the stairs.

GERRY Then who are we talking about?

LAURA Never mind. It doesn't matter.

GERRY No, hold on. Who are we talking about here? Not Stephanie, we've established that. We already know about Glyn. Not Adam, we think. Not me. Who does that leave us with, I wonder?

LAURA I don't know.

GERRY *(staring at her hard)* Who is it?

LAURA *appears not to hear him.*

(rising) Who is he, Laura?

She continues to ignore him.

(moving closer to her and bellowing) Laura, who the bloody hell is he?

For a second, he makes as if to hit her but as he does so she turns to face him fully. The expression on her face causes him to check the blow.

LAURA *(hissing at him with loathing)* Don't you dare. Don't you dare lay one finger on me...

At this moment, ERNESTO CALVINU *chooses to join them. He carries a tray with three small glasses and a bottle of his country's finest liqueur.*

CALVINU *(as he enters)* My friends... My good friends... Just in time for the end of the special birthday...

GERRY Ah!

LAURA Aha!

CALVINU I bring you a little something to toast. Some Schroopellick Crouscac. Literally, "Buds of the Little Blossoms". Delicious... *(He puts down the tray)*

LAURA How lovely.

GERRY Wonderful.

CALVINU *(kissing LAURA)* For the birthday girl...

LAURA Yes...

CALVINU *(slapping GERRY on the shoulder)* And her lucky, lucky birthday husband. *(He embraces GERRY warmly, then starts to pour out three glasses and distribute them)* A good meal? Yes?

GERRY Oh, yes. As always, Ernesto...

CALVINU A successful party?

LAURA Wonderful. *(She accepts a glass)* Thank you.

CALVINU Now this is special. Very special, special. From my own cellar. It is made only in my village.

GERRY Really?

LAURA Well...

CALVINU And it is the tradition, once the cork has left the bottle, it must never return. The bottle must be emptied.

GERRY Well, we'll do our best...

CALVINU Also. It must be drunk quickly. You must not sip. If you sip Schroopellick it is said a man loses his power and the woman loses her power over the man. Friends, your good health.

He drains his glass and looks at them expectantly. **GERRY** *sniffs his glass a little cautiously but* **LAURA,** *without a moment's hesitation, drains her glass in one gulp and slams it down on the table.*

LAURA Delicious.

GERRY *(following suit)* Very nice.

He sits back at the other end of the table from **LAURA.** *He likewise puts his glass down on the table. Their eyes meet like two gunfighters.*

CALVINU *(seating himself between them, unaware)* Dear friends, we have all the night, as we say, silently to listen to the wisdom of the wine...

As he starts to refill their glasses the lights dim on them slightly, but not entirely. Simultaneously they come up again on **ADAM** *and* **MAUREEN** *at the table downstage left. She has successfully polished off his pudding.*

MAUREEN That was delicious...

ADAM Listen, I was thinking... Just after Christmas, it's my mother's birthday and—

MAUREEN What date?

ADAM Er, the eighteenth of January...

MAUREEN Capricorn. She's a Capricorn. Just. On the cusp...

ADAM Oh, yes probably... Anyway, we usually have a sort of little party – well, not really a party – an informal supper here, in this restaurant – and I just wondered – I thought that might be a good occasion for you to meet them. I mean, it wouldn't be any big deal, it would just be casual. It wouldn't, you know, be me bringing you home to meet them or anything... I mean, you know...

MAUREEN (smiling at him tenderly) I know. I know what it'd be. Yes, I'd love to come. If you're sure that's all right?

ADAM Oh yes, that would be tremendous.

The lights come up on GLYN *and* STEPHANIE *at the table downstage left. The others also remain lit.*

GLYN (toasting her with his scotch) Here's to him, then...

STEPHANIE Or to her. It may be a her, this time.

GLYN That'd be nice. Her, then. Here's to her.

STEPHANIE (raising her water glass) Us.

GLYN Us.

CALVINU To love, to friendship, to long life...

LAURA Hear! Hear!

MAUREEN I wonder what I should wear...

The lights fade on all three couples to blackout.

ACT II

The same.

At the main table, it is a few minutes later. The bottle of Schroopellick is half empty. **LAURA** *and* **GERRY** *sit as before, two combatants biding their time in an unfinished, interrupted contest.* **CALVINU** *is blissfully unaware of them. The lateness of the hour and the drink have caused him to fall asleep. He is snoring gently. A silence. The ensuing conversation takes place in furious whispers.*

GERRY Who is it, then?

> **LAURA** *does not acknowledge him.* **CALVINU** *snores.*

(a shade louder) Who is he?

LAURA Sssshh!

GERRY *(softly again)* Who is he?

> *There is no reply.* **CALVINU** *snores.*

Laura!

LAURA There's no point in talking about it here, is there?

GERRY Now! I want to talk about it now...

LAURA How can we talk about it now?

> **CALVINU** *snores.*

GERRY All right. Come on, we're going home...

LAURA I haven't finished my drink...

GERRY *(furiously)* You heard me – home!

LAURA Don't you shout at me!

GERRY I'm not shouting at you. I wish to God I could.

LAURA Just calm down, calm down, will you. You'll drop dead in a minute.

CALVINU *snores.*

GERRY Don't worry, I won't be the one who drops dead. Have no fear about that. Whoever he is, he'll be the one that drops dead because I'll murder the bastard. I'll kill him and I'll thrash the living daylights out of you.

LAURA Oh, shut up. Big talk. Just shut up.

GERRY I promise. I will.

CALVINU *snores.*

LAURA You can't murder him, anyway.

GERRY Why not?

LAURA Because he's already dead, isn't he? He's been dead since nineteen seventy-four.

A silence. CALVINU *snores.*

Now simmer down... For God's sake.

Silence.

That's better.

GERRY I still want to know who he was.

LAURA What are you planning to do? Go round and beat up his kids?

GERRY His kids? Do you mean he was married as well?

LAURA Getting warmer.

CALVINU *snores.*

GERRY Who do we know who lost her husband in nineteen seventy-four?

The lights fade on them, as **CALVINU** *snores gently and* **GERRY** *furrows his brow.* **LAURA** *is surprisingly calm as she helps herself to more liqueur. The lights crossfade to* **ADAM** *and* **MAUREEN** *at their table, downstage left. For them it is three weeks earlier, the evening of Saturday, 30th November. They are both in the middle of their main courses – she with a fish dish, he with a meat course. She is not yet her full exotic self but a toned-down version of how she was on the date they had before this – the previous Saturday, which we shall see shortly. They are clearly deeply, passionately in love. They are eating but their eyes are fixed on each other.*

MAUREEN *(urgently)* I want to make love to you now.

ADAM Now?

MAUREEN Yes.

ADAM Here?

MAUREEN Yes. I want to take all your clothes off...and cover you in gravy...and lick, lick, lick—

ADAM *chokes.*

You all right?

ADAM *(weakly)* Yes...

MAUREEN Drink something... Something go down the wrong way...

ADAM *(drinking)* Yes, it's OK... Don't do that, not when I'm eating!

MAUREEN *growls.*

Now, cut that out. Shall I tell you what I'm going to do to you, then?

MAUREEN *(excitedly)* Yes, yes, yes, yes, yes—

ADAM As soon as I've finished my meal... I'll tell you...

MAUREEN Get the bill... We'll have pudding at home.

ADAM OK. *(He eats a little faster)*

MAUREEN Special pudding. Shaky pudding.

ADAM Careful. People are watching.

MAUREEN *(wiggling in her chair)* Shaky, shaky, shaky pud—

ADAM Oh, this is impossible – I can't finish this...

MAUREEN Good. That was the whole idea.

ADAM We've paid for all this and we've hardly eaten it...

MAUREEN I've paid for it – my turn. You paid last time. Again—

ADAM But—

MAUREEN We agreed. My turn. None of that.

ADAM Right.

MAUREEN *(making to rise)* Come on...

ADAM *(stopping her)* Mo—

MAUREEN Yes...?

ADAM I—

MAUREEN What is it?

ADAM I – just wanted to say – I hope we might – make this – sort of more permanent, you know.

MAUREEN Permanent?

ADAM Yes.

MAUREEN Us?

ADAM Yes. If you'd like that. I would. I'd like to think we could be together regularly.

MAUREEN Regularly?

ADAM Yes.

MAUREEN How regularly? You mean like now? Every Saturday?

ADAM No. Every day.

MAUREEN Every night?

ADAM Yes.

MAUREEN You mean like living together?

ADAM Yes – if you like. I thought... Here... *(He fumbles in his pocket and produces a small box)* Here—

MAUREEN What's that?

ADAM Here. *(He gives her the box)*

MAUREEN *(opening the box and staring at the contents)* Oh...

ADAM It's – it's not – it's not necessarily an engagement ring, you know. It's just a ring. For you. From me.

MAUREEN Yes. *(She studies it)* It looks a bit like an engagement ring to me.

ADAM Well, it could be. If you like. It's quite a nice one. It's second-hand.

MAUREEN That doesn't matter, I don't mind that. It's beautiful. I'll put it on, shall I?

ADAM If – if you want to...

MAUREEN Listen, if we're doing things properly, aren't you supposed to ask me something first, before I do...?

ADAM Oh – yes – er...

MAUREEN Don't worry, you don't have to kneel down...

ADAM Would you – er – would you – like – sort of to – get engaged – to...marry me? Would you?

MAUREEN Well. I'll need to think about it.

ADAM *(suddenly very anxious)* You will?

MAUREEN *(carefully)* Yes, you see, I have had several other offers, Adam—

ADAM *(crestfallen)* Have you?

MAUREEN that I never told you about. And to be fair to everyone concerned, I'll have to put your offer alongside theirs and then— *(She is unable to continue)* Oh God, your face – yes, of course I will.

ADAM You will?

MAUREEN Yes. Please. Please. Please. *(She kisses him)*

ADAM Oh, I'm so... I'm so... Oh, good. Here... *(He helps put the ring on her finger)* Come on. Home for pudding. I'll get the bill...

He starts off swiftly.

MAUREEN Hey, no wait... Adam! It's my turn. Don't you dare. Adam!

ADAM *has gone.*

(rescuing her bag from under the table) Oh, you bastard! *(She glances down at her hand, with realization)* Hey, he's put it on the wrong finger...

She smiles, then stops as a thought occurs to her. She stares at the ring again. She frowns, shrugs and goes off after him a little pensively.

The lights fade on their area and we return to GERRY, LAURA and CALVINU at the main table, a few minutes later. CALVINU snores. The others continue to whisper.

GERRY *(softly, as before)* Who the hell do we know who died in nineteen seventy-four...?

LAURA It's all over, it's dead and buried. He's dead and buried. It's over.

GERRY It's not over till I say it is.

LAURA I'm sorry I even mentioned it. Fifteen minutes in the back of his station wagon, I'm sorry I mentioned it.

GERRY *(loudly)* In the back of a station wagon...!

CALVINU *stirs in his sleep.*

LAURA Sssshhh!

GERRY *(quietly)* I don't believe this.

LAURA Nor did I at the time.

GERRY Who the hell do we know who was married, drove a station wagon and died in nineteen seventy-four...?

LAURA I was drunk, that's all, he got me drunk...

GERRY And who drank? Died in nineteen seventy-four – drank himself to death, maybe? Married – nineteen seventy-four – station wagon...?

CALVINU *(awakening with a shout)* Pedentaaay! Good health, friends! Good health! *(He becomes aware of his surroundings)* Ah! I was sleeping? Yes?

LAURA Yes.

CALVINU You should have woken me...

LAURA We didn't like to. You looked so peaceful.

CALVINU Sometimes, old friends – we are older than sometimes. Tonight – after a long day – I'm a hundred...

GERRY Yes, I know the feeling...

CALVINU It's been many years, eh?

LAURA Many years.

CALVINU Do you know how long I have had this restaurant?

LAURA A long time.

CALVINU Thirty-six years...

LAURA As long as that?

CALVINU *(sharing out the remainder of the liqueur)* I start it thirty-six years ago with my wife Taisa – you remember Taisa...

LAURA Yes, I do...She was beautiful...

CALVINU Ran away with the man from the town hall. Comes to inspect my kitchen, runs away with my wife...

LAURA Yes, I remember...

CALVINU And my cousin was the chef. Rootzer. You remember my cousin Rootzer? Big Rootzer?

LAURA Oh, yes...

CALVINU God rest his soul—

GERRY *(suspiciously)* What year did he die...?

CALVINU Oh, nineteen seventy-eight, nine... Long time ago. You, my friends, were practically my first customers...

LAURA We were.

CALVINU You courted in here... You were nearly married here, eh? You bring your children here, your family. Your big boys now. They still come here with their women...

LAURA Yes.

CALVINU All your family. Your sister from America. She come here.

LAURA Anthea. Yes, she did.

CALVINU *(to GERRY)* And your brother – David? It was David, yes...?

LAURA David, yes.

CALVINU He was also here—

LAURA Yes.

CALVINU Ah, so sad. The cruelty of the wine. It can be a friend but it can also be your worst enemy. For a man to die like that – so young, so handsome – in that cruel way – to leave his wife, his children, all his loved ones, his dear brother...

GERRY *(dead)* David.

CALVINU *(startled by his tone)* My friend?

GERRY David.

CALVINU I'm sorry, I should not have—

GERRY *(incredulously)* David? David? *(With a cry)* DAVID?

GERRY rushes out.

CALVINU I'm sorry, I shouldn't... I have upset him, I'm sorry... I should not have mentioned David.

LAURA No. It brings back painful memories for him...

CALVINU I know. I'm sorry. It was thoughtless. *(He shakes his head)* I must cash up. I will see he's all right, don't worry.

He goes, leaving LAURA alone at the table. She sips her drink and waits.

The lights crossfade to STEPHANIE, who sits alone at her table, downstage right. For her it is lunch time on Friday, 24th July that same year. She is six-and-a-half months pregnant and, despite her capacious, loose-flowing maternity clothes, is hot and uncomfortable. She is picking her way through her main course, a salad dish of some description. To accompany it she has a bottle of mineral water. She fans herself with the menu and looks out of the window.

In time, GLYN hurtles in and sits down opposite her. He is hot and breathless. His jacket is off and his tie loosened.

STEPHANIE Where have you been?

GLYN I'm sorry.

STEPHANIE Where have you been?

GLYN Oh, you have started. Good.

STEPHANIE I've been here since one o'clock, it's ten to two, where have you been?

GLYN Where do you think?

STEPHANIE In the office?

GLYN Obviously. Where else would I be?

STEPHANIE I don't know. I wonder, sometimes. I phoned. They said you weren't there...

GLYN When was this?

STEPHANIE About twenty to one. I phoned to say I might be five minutes late. They said you weren't there. You'd gone out.

GLYN Oh, yes, I was – I popped down to the site. She should have told you that. The girl's a half-wit.

STEPHANIE She must be. She said you'd been out since eleven.

GLYN What does she know?

STEPHANIE I don't know. More than I do, probably.

GLYN Oh, come on. Don't start that. No more of that.

STEPHANIE All right.

GLYN That's ridiculous. You're being stupid. Now stop it, do you hear.

STEPHANIE I'm sorry. *(She rummages in her bag and changes the subject abruptly)* There was a postcard from your mother. Arrived just after you left. I thought you'd like to see it.

GLYN Oh, was there? That's nice. *(Vainly)* Waiter—

STEPHANIE Here. *(She hands him the card)*

GLYN *(studying the picture)* Oh, look at that. Doesn't it look beautiful? Lucky thing. Dive straight into that today, couldn't you?

STEPHANIE Yes.

GLYN *reads the postcard, chuckling now and then.*

Picked a great time to be pregnant, haven't I? Bang in the middle of a heat wave...

GLYN *(not looking up)* How you feeling?

STEPHANIE Like a big wet elephant. Picked a wonderful time...

GLYN Well, to be fair, I don't think it was us who really picked it, did we?

STEPHANIE No. You're right. We didn't. It picked us. Nothing to do with us...

GLYN *(not really hearing her as he finishes reading the card)* Oh, that's great, isn't it? She really seems to be enjoying herself, doesn't she?

STEPHANIE Yes, she does.

GLYN I know she's my mother and I shouldn't say it, but she's a remarkable woman really, isn't she?

STEPHANIE How do you mean?

GLYN Well, look at her. The old man's been buried – what? – barely six months. For over thirty years they were inseparable. Close as that. And somehow or other she's managed to put it all behind her. Pick herself up, get back on her feet, carry on, start a new life. Now, that takes real bottle, if you ask me. That shows true character.

STEPHANIE You're going to have to do the same, starting next week, aren't you?

GLYN Right. Dead right. New boss. New job, new title.

STEPHANIE Is it going to be very different?

GLYN What, the business, you mean? No, I can't see them making any sweeping changes. Not to Stratton's. I mean, we're basically – in their terms anyway – a smallish but highly efficient business. I mean, we've had a few hiccups in the last few months but who hasn't lately? Who? I reckon they're going to leave us very much alone, if you ask me. I mean, my job won't change. Not essentially. Not a jot.

STEPHANIE I see. They're not going to get rid of you then?

GLYN Get rid of me? How do you mean?

STEPHANIE Well, with being taken over, I thought—

GLYN I'd like to see them try. Whole bloody place would grind to a halt if they did. I mean, we have men who've worked there all their lives. First for Dad and latterly for me. Absolute solid, unswerving loyalty. None of that boss-employee business. First-name terms, these lads. Try and get rid of me, they'd have them all out. Anyway, it's not that sort of take-over. Don't worry. Where's the bloody waiter? This place is getting worse, you know... We'll have to stop eating here. It's gone right downhill.

STEPHANIE Oh, Adam phoned. They can't come to dinner next Thursday.

GLYN No? Oh, that's a pity. Why's that?

STEPHANIE Well... Actually, I don't think he and Maureen are together any more. That's the main reason.

GLYN (not that upset) No? Oh, dear. They were getting on so well. What went wrong? I thought he'd really cracked it this time. They were practically engaged, weren't they?

STEPHANIE They were engaged...

GLYN Well, not officially. Not according to Mother, they weren't.

STEPHANIE Maureen seemed to think it was official, but I agree there was a slight difference of opinion...

GLYN Well, what's gone wrong?

STEPHANIE I don't know. He wants to come round and talk about it. He's very upset.

GLYN Oh, poor old Adam. Poor lad. Listen, we ought to take him out somewhere, somewhere quiet, let him pour it all out to us, get it off his chest. Probably nothing serious.

STEPHANIE No, he wants to talk to me on his own. He doesn't want you there.

GLYN *(hurt)* Oh. OK. Fair enough. The woman's touch, eh? Let me know if I can help in any way...

STEPHANIE I will.

GLYN Remind him of the old saying: if your personal life collapses, throw yourself into your work...

STEPHANIE Glyn, he's unemployed...

GLYN He's got plans, though. What about his recording studio idea?

STEPHANIE What about it?

GLYN No?

STEPHANIE What do you think?

GLYN Well, I don't know. He never sticks at things, that's half his trouble, if you ask me... Waiter!

  DINKA *appears.*

DINKA What you want?

GLYN At last! I want to order, what do you think?

DINKA What you want to order?

GLYN I don't know. I haven't seen a bloody menu yet, have I?

STEPHANIE Glyn—

DINKA You want a menu?

GLYN Yes, of course I want a menu.

DINKA Then, I get you a menu.

GLYN Oh, don't bother. What's the special today?

DINKA Slookick with rice, onion and fresh herb...

GLYN That'll do. Give me some of that.

DINKA It's all gone.

GLYN Oh, God in heaven. Get me a menu, then.

DINKA I get you a menu.

GLYN This place has gone right off, I tell you. This is the very last time we come here.

> *The lights fade on them as he glares round and* **STEPHANIE** *continues to toy with her lettuce leaf. The lights return to* **ADAM** *and* **MAUREEN**, *who are back at their table. It is Saturday evening, 23rd November, virtually their first proper date together since their initial meeting a week ago. They are both rather on their best behaviour. He has settled for somewhat conventional clothes, a jacket and tie, presumably to reflect her style of dress of the previous week. This time, though, she has opted for the full, exotic works. A veritable, ultra-modern bird of paradise. She's carrying it off with a certain aplomb, despite feeling a little ill-matched with her partner. They are eating their first course now – she, chopped fruit of some description and he, some thick soup. A slight pause while they eat.*

ADAM Is that all right? What you ordered?

MAUREEN Yes, it's very, very nice, thank you. Extremely pleasant.

ADAM Good. This is nice.

MAUREEN It looks nice.

ADAM Yes, it is.

> *Pause. They eat.*

It's a sort of soup.

MAUREEN Yes.

ADAM Vegetable. I think.

MAUREEN Yes. It looks delicious.

They eat.

This is sort of fruit.

ADAM Yes.

MAUREEN I'm not sure what sort, though.

ADAM I'll ask them. If you like. I'll ask them.

MAUREEN It could be melon but it tastes a bit like pineapple. I think there's melon in it, but there's something else as well with it.

ADAM Could be pineapple.

MAUREEN Yes, it could well be pineapple...

ADAM Or perhaps lychees?

MAUREEN Cheese?

ADAM No, lychees. It's a Chinese fruit...

MAUREEN Oh, yes. No. I've had lychees. In the Chinese.

ADAM *(knowledgeably)* Yes. That's where you tend to get them.

MAUREEN I don't like them, actually. I always think I'm eating eyeballs.

ADAM Really?

MAUREEN Or something similar...

ADAM What?

MAUREEN *(embarrassed)* Nothing...

ADAM Sorry?

MAUREEN *(covered in confusion)* Sorry. Nothing. Just my mind.

He smiles at her. She attempts to regain her dignity. They eat.

ADAM You look really – very – very attractive. If you don't mind me saying...

MAUREEN Oh, thank you.

ADAM Terrific. I hardly recognized you.

MAUREEN Well. I thought I'd make an effort.

ADAM Yes.

MAUREEN One of the girls in the salon, she did it for me last night. The hair.

ADAM Must have taken a bit of time.

MAUREEN It did. Hours. Specially with my hair.

ADAM Really?

MAUREEN Had to sleep last night with my neck on a plank...

ADAM A plank?

MAUREEN Well, a board. You know.

ADAM A board?

MAUREEN A wooden board, you know. To stop it getting flattened.

ADAM Stop what getting flattened?

MAUREEN My hair.

ADAM Oh, I see. *(He ponders)* Do you have it done like that very often, then?

MAUREEN No, not very often...

ADAM *(secretly relieved)* Ah.

MAUREEN Only when I'm going out somewhere.

ADAM Ah.

MAUREEN But I don't go out much.

ADAM You were out last week.

MAUREEN Pardon?

ADAM You were out last week. Here.

MAUREEN Yes, I know...

ADAM But you weren't dressed like that—

MAUREEN No, well. That was a blind date, wasn't it? I didn't
know who this Robin man was, did I? You don't want to
go to a lot of trouble for someone they've fished out of a
computer you don't know from – *(She laughs)* That's quite
funny. I was going to say – you don't know from Adam.
That's quite funny, isn't it? Adam. You get it?

ADAM I'm – I'm glad you think I'm worth it...

MAUREEN *(affably)* Well. We'll have to see, won't we? Worth
the risk.

Pause. They eat.

ADAM Er... Where'd you get the plank?

MAUREEN Pardon?

ADAM The plank you had to sleep on. Where'd you get it?

MAUREEN It was my bookshelf.

ADAM Oh. What did you do with the books?

MAUREEN Put them on the floor.

ADAM Ah.

MAUREEN I've only got three.

ADAM Oh.

MAUREEN I prefer magazines, really.

A pause. They eat.

My dad put it up for me.

ADAM Sorry?

MAUREEN The shelf.

ADAM Your dad? The racing driver?

MAUREEN No, he's not a racing driver.

ADAM He's not? I thought...?

MAUREEN I only said that. I was just trying to impress you. I thought it sounded more interesting.

ADAM Oh. What does he do then?

MAUREEN He's a brickie.

ADAM Oh.

MAUREEN But he's not working regular. That's why he builds shelves. Whenever he's laid off at home my mother makes him build shelves. We've got thousands of shelves everywhere in our house. She's got a thing about shelves, my mother. Shoves everything on shelves. Shove me on a shelf if she could. *(Pause)* She's not an ex-ballet dancer either. In case you're wondering. *(Pause)* But she does work.

ADAM Where's that?

MAUREEN Tesco's.

ADAM Aha. Maybe that's why she's so fond of shelves...

MAUREEN Pardon?

ADAM Nothing.

MAUREEN No, she's on the tills.

ADAM Right.

They finish their first courses.

MAUREEN Did you find that person you were looking for last week? The one you needed for your office?

ADAM No, not yet. I'm seeing one or two more on Monday.

MAUREEN I hope you're not planning to take them all out to dinner here.

ADAM Oh no. It was only that particular one. She was very experienced. It would have been quite something to have got her...

MAUREEN Did you manage to catch up with her?

ADAM No – she's...not answering my calls.

MAUREEN Probably fed up having to pay for her own dinner.

ADAM Oh no, I'm sure she... Anyway, we were offering so little she probably wouldn't have been interested.

MAUREEN What do you do in your office?

ADAM We – we've just started a magazine. Sort of arts magazine for this area. Reviews. Articles, interviews. There's a lot going on. Masses. The local press just aren't interested most of the time. Lot of talent around. You'd be surprised. We thought we'd try and encourage it.

MAUREEN Right. Do people buy it? The magazine?

ADAM Well. We need more to keep going. But we've started well. We're six per cent above our budgeted circulation figures. Oh, look... *(He produces a crumpled, cheaply produced magazine)* I brought you volume two. In case you wanted to have a look. Here. It's for you.

MAUREEN *(gingerly taking it)* Thank you. *(She puts it straight in her bag)* I'll read it. Put it on my shelf. Would you like me to pay for it?

ADAM Oh, no. Complimentary edition. Please.

MAUREEN Thank you. Incidentally, I am paying for this evening, though...

ADAM Oh, no please. I insist...

MAUREEN No, you paid last week. Fair's fair.

ADAM All right. We'll see.

Pause.

MAUREEN *(looking around)* It's not bad this place. Not too stuffy. You come here a lot?

ADAM Yes, it's my parents' favourite restaurant. We used to come here as kids. They used to bring us.

MAUREEN Us?

ADAM My brother and I. My older brother, Glyn.

MAUREEN You like to go where your parents go, do you?

ADAM Not always, no.

MAUREEN Is your brother married?

ADAM Oh, yes.

MAUREEN Has he got any children?

ADAM Yes. One.

MAUREEN How old—?

ADAM *(vaguely)* Oh, about four. Or so. A boy. Timothy. Timmy.

MAUREEN You're an uncle, then?

ADAM Right.

MAUREEN What does he do, your brother? Does he run arty magazines, as well?

ADAM Oh no. He's with our firm. With my father's firm.

MAUREEN What do they do?

ADAM *(slightly uncomfortable)* Well, we were originally builders but we're also transport and we build leisure centres...

MAUREEN Big, then?

ADAM Pretty big. I don't have anything to do with it.

MAUREEN What do they call themselves?

ADAM Er... Stratton's... Stratton Unity...

MAUREEN Stratton's?

ADAM Yes.

MAUREEN What, *the* Stratton's?

ADAM Yes.

MAUREEN Hang on, that's your name, isn't it?

ADAM Yes. Adam Stratton, yes.

MAUREEN And you own that?

ADAM No, I don't. My family does. My father.

MAUREEN You must be rolling—

ADAM Oh, no. Well, they are. I'm not.

MAUREEN They're massive. Stratton's. Huge.

ADAM Pretty big.

MAUREEN Bloody hell. Why am I offering to pay for your dinner? *(She studies him)* I didn't realize I was out with a Stratton.

ADAM Well...

MAUREEN If you don't mind me saying so, you could afford a better jacket, couldn't you?

ADAM Oh, don't you...?

MAUREEN It's terrible. Even my dad wouldn't be seen dead in that.

ADAM I'm sorry...

MAUREEN It's all right. I didn't come out with you for your jacket... *(She smiles)*

ADAM *smiles.*

Which is just as well. And I didn't come out because you were rich, either, because I didn't know who you were when I said yes and it wouldn't have made any difference even if I had done and I'm still paying half...

ADAM Fair enough. And I'm not rich. You don't get rich running arts magazines.

MAUREEN Amaze me with some more little known facts.

AGGI *returns to clear their plates.*

AGGI Madametta... Seerar... You finish? You enjoy? Yes?

MAUREEN Very much. Thank you?

ADAM We wanted to know, what was the fruit? The lady's fruit?

AGGI The lady's fruit? It is – er...melon...

MAUREEN Melon, yes. I got that one.

AGGI With some – pine-apple...

MAUREEN Pineapple. Yes, I said it was pineapple...

AGGI And the juice of – er...passion fruit.

MAUREEN Passion fruit?

AGGI It's good, eh? It's good for tonight? Passion fruit?

MAUREEN I don't know about that. He's a bit cheeky, isn't he?

ADAM Oh, don't mind him, he's always—

AGGI *(bursting into a loud, full-blooded love ballad)*
Tennesta limpa
... Consensa far ma plea
... Inento! ...inento! ...inento!

MAUREEN *(during this)* He's mad, as well.

ADAM No, he's...

MAUREEN I feel stupid—

As **AGGI** *finishes his recital, on bended knee, he presents* **MAUREEN** *with a flower from the vase on their table.*

Thank you. Thank you very much.

AGGI Deveena Madametta – pulchrosia...

MAUREEN Lovely, yes. Hell, I'm not coming here again—

AGGI Passion fruit! I fetch your main course.

ADAM Please.

AGGI *goes off with the empty dishes.*

Sorry about that.

MAUREEN It's all right, really. It was funny, really. You say your family have been coming here for years?

ADAM Oh, yes. Since before I was born.

MAUREEN You must have a funny family, then.

ADAM Yes. Fairly funny. Sometimes.

MAUREEN I'd like to meet them. You know, just to meet them. Not – you know.

ADAM Yes. Maybe. I mean—

MAUREEN I don't have to look like this... I mean, if you think that would frighten them—

ADAM No. Of course not—

MAUREEN I've got a proper dress somewhere. My mother bought it me. A really boring one, I promise. It'd go with your jacket.

ADAM I'm burning this tomorrow.

MAUREEN No, don't. I like it really. It reminds me of our dog's blanket.

ADAM Oh, leave it out...

MAUREEN Sorry.

ADAM You have a dog?

MAUREEN No, just a blanket.

ADAM Ah.

MAUREEN He got run over. But my mother's sentimental. She still keeps his blanket.

ADAM On a shelf?

MAUREEN *(laughing)* Where else?

> *They both laugh. Suddenly she leans forward and kisses him lightly on the lips. She sits back. They look at each other.*

Oh well. The night is young, as they say.

ADAM It is.

MAUREEN Haven't got to the pud yet, have we?

> *They continue to smile at each other as the lights fade on them. Simultaneously we return to the main table where* **LAURA** *is still seated. Half an hour has passed.*
>
> **GERRY** *returns slowly. His manner is subdued. He sits at the table.*

LAURA *(after a second)* Where have you been?

GERRY For a walk. I needed some air.

LAURA You've been gone ages. I thought you'd drowned yourself.

GERRY I might have done. I could well have done.

LAURA Oh, don't be so melodramatic.

GERRY I've reason to be, haven't I? I discover, after thirty-two years, my whole marriage is based on a lie. I've been betrayed by my wife – with my own brother... My whole personal life been made a mockery—

LAURA *(impatiently)* Oh, for God's sake. Fifteen minutes. That's all it was. In nineteen seventy-four. A month before he died, poor bugger. From the little pleasure we had from it, it probably helped him on his way.

GERRY God, you're a cold woman sometimes, aren't you?

LAURA It's the truth. Come on, don't be so stupid. It was nothing.

GERRY Then why bother telling me if it was nothing?

LAURA I don't know. I thought it might amuse you.

GERRY *(outraged)* Amuse me?

LAURA Well, it was long enough ago. *(She laughs)* It was very funny, actually...

GERRY *(angrily)* I don't want to hear! You think it's a joke? It's not a joke.

LAURA No, all right. I'm sorry.

GERRY It may be a joke for you. I have to face people tomorrow, you know.

LAURA What are you talking about?

GERRY People sniggering behind their hands.

LAURA Don't be so stupid. How can they, they don't even know about it.

GERRY How do I know that for certain?

LAURA Well, I've never told anyone except you, and you've only just heard about it and he's dead so who else is there?

GERRY Did no one see you? You know...doing it?

LAURA Of course they didn't.

GERRY Where did it happen? Where was this station wagon parked?

LAURA I thought you didn't want to hear—

GERRY Where?

LAURA Holly Lane.

GERRY Holly Lane?

LAURA Back of the social club. In the members' car park.

GERRY Oh, my God! Our own social club. *(He calms down)* In that case, how can you be sure no one saw you?

LAURA They didn't. We'd have heard about it by now if they had.

GERRY Was it very dark?

LAURA It wasn't dark at all, it was lunch time.

GERRY Lunch time!

LAURA Sunday.

GERRY Sunday lunch time? Where was I during all this, then?

LAURA In the club bar.

GERRY I see.

LAURA Drawing the cricket club raffle—

GERRY I see. And there's a lull in the proceedings so you two both went out there and then and had it, did you?

LAURA Well, he asked me first.

GERRY That was decent of him. Always the gentleman, my brother. What did he say?

LAURA *(vaguely)* He said, "Come on, what about it?" I think. Something like that. He was never one for speeches, David, was he?

GERRY Man of few words?

LAURA Right.

GERRY Quite a bit of action, though.

LAURA *(drily)* Not a lot of that either, as I remember. Poor man.

GERRY *(weakly)* I don't know what to say.

LAURA Come on, what's the matter with you? Once in thirty-two years. Come on. Hardly makes me Jezebel, does it?

GERRY You say once. How do I know that?

LAURA Because I never lie to you. I never have.

GERRY You lied to me about him, didn't you? About David?

LAURA No, I didn't. I just never told you about him at all. That's not the same as lying.

GERRY Don't play with words. Don't try and get clever with me.

LAURA There's been no one else. Ever. All right?

GERRY Well, I can't believe you. I'm sorry.

LAURA *(suddenly furious)* Then you're a bloody fool, aren't you? That's all. If you knew how faithful I've been to you over the years... Oh no, not just sexually – but that as well – standing up for you time after time, fighting your corner even when I knew you were in the wrong... And you just took it, as if it was yours by right. Your right that I'd always be there whenever I was wanted, saying what I was expected to say, doing what I was expected to do. And never once – Well, bugger you, that's all I can say, bugger you!

Silence. They are both a little surprised by her outburst.

(quietly) And I'm sorry for swearing.

LAURA *rises suddenly, taking up her handbag and scrabbling inside for a tissue. It is apparent she is about to cry but doesn't want to do so in front of him.*

GERRY Where you going?

LAURA To the Ladies' room. *(She turns, rather tearful now)* You wouldn't even let me have a dog, would you? You know how much I love dogs...

LAURA *exits.*

GERRY *(muttering to himself)* I hate bloody dogs...

*He continues to sit there, thoughtful, as the lights fade on the main table and come up on **GLYN** and **STEPHANIE**'s table, downstage right. It is again lunch time, this time on Friday, 6th November. **STEPHANIE** is, as usual, at the table on her own. This time, though, there is evidence that she has not been eating alone and that **GLYN** has simply slipped away for a second. **STEPHANIE** has had her second child but she has failed to regain much of her figure. She looks a mess, post-natally depressed, neglected*

*by others and herself. The pair have all but finished
their meal – poised between main course and sweets.*

A moment and then GLYN *returns. He has been on the
phone and has his Filofax in hand.*

GLYN OK. All settled. She'll be here in ten minutes. She'll pick
me up, take me back to the house. I can be packed and out
of there in half an hour, before you get home. No trace. OK?

STEPHANIE *(dead)* Good.

GLYN Now, this is what we agreed, all right? This is what we
both want.

STEPHANIE Right.

GLYN I'm not doing anything that we haven't agreed on between
us. Right?

STEPHANIE Right.

GLYN It's best for you, it's best for the kids, it's best for me—

STEPHANIE And best for her.

GLYN I don't think she enters into this, do you—

STEPHANIE Oh, I think she probably does, you know.

GLYN *(determinedly ignoring her sarcasm)* It's not like I'm
leaving. I'm not walking out on you. I am not abandoning
you. I gave my word on that and I stand by my word. I
am still there when you need me, at the end of the phone,
night or day, rain or shine. And you come first, Steph. You
know that. You and Timmy and little Jess will always come
first. I have made that crystal clear to Sarah. She is strictly
number two in the pecking order—

STEPHANIE Number four...

GLYN What's that?

STEPHANIE Number four. You said she was number two. She's
number four in the pecking order.

GLYN *(slightly impatiently)* All right then, number two, number four, have it your way, who's counting? The fact is, if the crunch comes, she waits strictly in line. She knows that—

STEPHANIE Poor thing—

GLYN *(admonishingly)* Now, Steph...

STEPHANIE Sorry.

GLYN Don't spoil it now. We're handling this well between us. We both are. Don't spoil it.

TUTO *enters.*

TUTO Madama, seerar. You want a sweet? You want to see the sweet trolley?

GLYN Not just at the moment, thanks.

TUTO You want just coffee?

GLYN In a minute.

TUTO OK.

TUTO *goes off again.*

GLYN Now, is there anything you want me to do before I go?

STEPHANIE No.

GLYN You got my number?

STEPHANIE Yes.

GLYN And you're not to worry about money, either. I won't keep you short. You'll probably find you're better off, anyway, without me to worry about. Well, it may get a bit tight, I admit, for a week or two – until I've got this problem at work sorted out... But there's no way they're going to treat me like that and get away with it. I am demanding full compensation and I intend to fight them till I get it. And I don't mean an offer of a so-called golden handshake where all I finish up with is two fingers. No, we'll survive, never fear. There's a lot of people showing interest in me at the moment. Word's got round I'm on the market. I'm not going to be short of offers, don't worry. Some of these little firms, they'd give anything to get a Stratton on their board... Boost their credibility no end.

STEPHANIE *(dully)* Your mother's back, did you know? She phoned me last night.

GLYN Yes. I was going to tell you that. I popped up to see her this morning.

STEPHANIE With *her*?

GLYN What?

STEPHANIE Did you go up to see your mother with *her*?

GLYN *(as casually as he can)* Yes, as a matter of fact Sarah was with me, yes.

STEPHANIE Didn't your mother think that was odd? You coming to see her with Sarah?

GLYN Well, she didn't remark on it – but you know my mother, she's very discreet—

STEPHANIE *laughs.*

She asked after you. How you were.

STEPHANIE Oh, that's nice.

GLYN Wanted to know how Timmy was. How much he'd grown since she's been away. And of course she's desperate to see little Jess.

STEPHANIE I bet.

GLYN You'll try and get up to see her, won't you?

STEPHANIE Maybe.

GLYN Well, you've got the car, Steph, haven't you? I left you with the car, for God's sake. Think about me. No car at all.

STEPHANIE You'll have to make do with her car then, won't you?

GLYN *(laughing)* I don't know about that. I think my days with open top convertibles are strictly numbered. *(Sincerely)* Do try to get up to see Mother, Steph. It would mean a lot to her, it really would. She's looking great by the way. Fantastic sun-tan. Had her hair re-coloured. Looks about twenty years younger. I said to her, you're back in with a chance, Mum.

STEPHANIE *(murmuring)* Lucky man.

GLYN Lucky man, yes. *(He looks around)* Must keep an eye out for Sarah. I don't know if she'll come in here or park outside... Oh, Adam was there, too. Saw him briefly.

STEPHANIE He's back home with her again, is he?

GLYN Yes. Temporarily. Mum's thrilled to bits, of course. Her chance to spoil him. He's talking of going to night school. To study architecture.

STEPHANIE Architecture?

GLYN I said, good for him, the way things are going at the moment I could do with a good cheap house... *(He catches sight of someone)* Ah! Here she is. OK. *(He rises)* As I say, I'll be in and out in half an hour. I'll just take my clothes, my personal things. Everything else is yours, OK? As we promised.

STEPHANIE Right.

GLYN Don't bother about the bill, I'll... *(Suddenly moved)* You've been amazing, Steph. Absolutely amazing over all this. Thank you. I won't forget it. I mean it. Thank you.

He considers kissing her but, realizing this might be altogether too much, finishes by giving her an affectionate pat on the shoulder. Then he is gone.

STEPHANIE *sits frozen, expressionless.*

In a moment, TUTO *returns with the sweet trolley.*

TUTO *(cheerfully)* Where's seerar? He's gone?

STEPHANIE *nods.*

You want to wait for him?

STEPHANIE *shakes her head.*

He's coming back?

STEPHANIE *shakes her head.*

You want a sweet?

STEPHANIE *nods.*

What you like? We have the specialities. Smooliboos. That is cream with meringue?

STEPHANIE *nods.*

OK, you like that? *(He starts to serve)* You want something with it? Something else? Some delicious trickletasse? This is delicious tart with treacle and cream mixed with passion fruit, fresh strawberries and Armagnac...?

STEPHANIE *nods. She begins to cry quietly.*

(oblivious to this) Yes, OK. Some trickletasse. What else can we tempt you? Some profiteroles? Some lemon mousse? Some fruit salad?

STEPHANIE *continues to nod automatically.*

You want some of those as well? What, all of them? My God, lady – when you last eat...? *(He ladles things on to the plate)* OK. Profiteroles...and some lemon mousse...and a little fruit salad...wow! You want cream? *(Before she can reply)* Of course you want cream. *(He places the plate in front of her)* Madama! Benzay appertass... Madama?

He notices for the first time that she is crying. Her sobs now become louder and slowly more convulsive.

(alarmed) Madama? *(Gently)* It's OK. It's OK. Don't cry now. It's OK. I get a doctor, OK? You'll be OK, OK? OK. *(Calling)* Bengie! Chetti Seerar Calvinu – telephon medicanti – medicanti – medicanti, yeah.

TUTO *returns to* **STEPHANIE.**

It's all right. Someone's coming. It's OK.

He touches her arm to console her. **STEPHANIE** *in her desolation, though still seated, turns and clings to him, burying her face in his jacket and continuing to weep.* **TUTO,** *rather embarrassed, stands patting her ineffectually.*

It's OK. It's OK. It's OK.

The lights fade on them and rise on the main table, where **GERRY** *is still seated. Five minutes or so have passed.*

LAURA *returns.*

LAURA Well, have you calmed down, then?

GERRY *(indignantly)* Me?

LAURA I hope you have.

Slight pause. **LAURA** *sits.*

We ought to go, you know. I think they're wanting to close up.

GERRY Did you really think it wouldn't matter to me? Telling me about you and David?

LAURA Well, does it?

GERRY Of course it does.

LAURA Oh, come on. It isn't as if we're great lovers, is it?

GERRY Maybe we aren't now, not now. But in nineteen seventy-four we were.

LAURA We weren't.

GERRY In nineteen seventy-four we were still—

LAURA We were not.

GERRY What are you talking about?

LAURA We bought single beds in August nineteen seventy. It's engraved on my memory. I remember saying to myself, goodbye the swinging sixties...

GERRY Nineteen seventy?

LAURA August the twenty-first, nineteen seventy. Friday.

GERRY Have you written all this down?

LAURA You remember these things. I do.

GERRY We bought single beds because of your back.

LAURA That was the official reason given at the time.

GERRY We've made love since nineteen seventy, for God's sake.

LAURA Oh, yes. On and off. But we're not great lovers, that's what I'm saying. There's not some burning passion where we can't bear to be out of each other's sight. We don't go mad with jealousy every time we see one of us talking to someone else who's half-way attractive.

GERRY We did. We used to—

LAURA Oh, we did... There's one or two of them nearly finished up in a bin liner, I can tell you... Girls after you.

GERRY Really? I didn't know about this...

LAURA No, you didn't...

GERRY Who were these, then?

LAURA Nevermind.

GERRY And you saw them off?

LAURA Oh, yes.

GERRY How'd you do that?

LAURA There are ways. A quiet word in the toilet and a bottle of nail polish remover...works wonders.

GERRY *(impressed)* Bloody hell! You did that? For me?

LAURA We were only kids...

GERRY You loved me that much?

LAURA I wanted you that much.

GERRY But you did love me?

LAURA At that time, I just wanted you. I was far too frightened of you then to love you...

GERRY Frightened?

LAURA Oh, yes. You were a frightening young man. Leader of the pack, you. King of the Teds, weren't you?

GERRY Teddy Boy King. Right. Remember those shoes? That thick, the soles were.

LAURA I remember the hair-do.

GERRY God, what a sight. What did you see in me?

LAURA *(a fond memory)* You were – dangerous. So dangerous.

GERRY Never.

LAURA Oh, you were. I remember those first few times you took me out. I nearly wet myself I was so frightened.

GERRY Of me?

LAURA Yes.

GERRY Why?

LAURA I don't know.

GERRY Then why did you come out with me?

LAURA Because I loved it. I loved every terrifying minute of it.

GERRY But you didn't love me?

LAURA Not then. Later. When I realized you were really a softy.

GERRY I loved you.

LAURA Yes, I know you did.

Slight pause.

Anyway – how did we get on to all that, for God's sake—? All I was saying was...we've both moved on. There's nothing wrong in that, it's called a marriage... We're no longer lovers – we're...

GERRY We're what?

LAURA We're a partnership.

GERRY You make it sound like a business arrangement.

LAURA Well, it is in a way – God, you men, you're so bloody romantic, aren't you? – of course it's a business. Partly. I hope there's more to it than just that but it's an important side of it, isn't it? It's a legal arrangement. It's a contract. We entered into it, we traded and in due course we diversified—

GERRY Diversified?

LAURA We had the boys...and then they occupied our attention... Our interest became largely in them, instead. Or, in my case, I have to confess, in Adam. You know how I feel about Glyn.

GERRY Yes, I do. But I don't pretend to understand it. Your own son.

LAURA I've never hidden it. Well, I've tried to from him, obviously, but... I don't know. There's no logical reason why parents should automatically love their children, is there? Really? I couldn't stand him when he was born. And now he's grown up thoroughly dull and conventional, no creativity, no scrap of imagination – he's always had everything he wanted – thanks to you – and he thinks the world owes him a living. He's treated that marriage of his like a one-night stand—

GERRY I don't think you can blame him entirely—

LAURA Oh, I don't. He chooses to marry a girl like Stephanie he gets what he deserves. She's as selfish as he is and hasn't got a brain in her head. She can't even cook, they have to eat out half the time. But I told him, he picked her, he sticks with her... Those are the rules. He might as well do one thing right in his life. We stuck by them, why shouldn't he?

GERRY Well. At least we have a grandchild. She's given us that.

LAURA Yes, well that's nice for you, anyway.

GERRY And for you?

> **LAURA** *doesn't answer.*

Having Timmy? That's nice for you too, isn't it?

LAURA You know how I feel about babies. I managed with my own – just...

GERRY You like them on television—

LAURA I love them on television. It's having to hold them in the flesh. Oh, don't worry, I'll come into my own with Timmy when he's about fifteen – if I'm still around, that is.

GERRY You may not love him but Glyn loves you, you know.

LAURA Really?

GERRY Much more than he does me. He needs your approval, Laura. He always needs that.

LAURA That's not quite the same as loving me, is it? Anyway, we can't change the way we are. I can't pretend to love him if I don't, can I? Now, Adam I do love. I understand him. And I think he loves me... He's a fool, sometimes, but at least I understand him.

GERRY I'm glad you do.

LAURA And I can still be of use to him, I know I can. He's got something, that boy. Real potential. And I'm going to make sure he gets the chance to realize it. Doesn't get trapped by some ambitious little nobody, like that one.

GERRY Now, be fair. How do you know she's that...?

LAURA Because I recognize her. From thirty years ago... Nothing changes.

GERRY What're you going to do, then? Have a quiet word with a bottle of acetone?

LAURA *(as if she means it)* If need be.

A silence. **GERRY** *stares at her.*

(without moving) We must go.

GERRY Just finish this off.

LAURA You're driving.

GERRY So what? Nothing on the road, this time of night.

He refills his glass. They sit in silence. The lights cross-fade to **MAUREEN,** *who is sitting at her table downstage right on her own. It is now the Saturday, 16th November of the previous year.* **MAUREEN** *has a pre-dinner drink but has yet to order. She is dressed very conventionally for her. She wears a red flower prominently in her jacket button hole.*

DINKA, *who, unfortunately for her, seems to be her waiter for the evening, enters with a menu.*

DINKA *(as gracelessly as ever)* You want to order?

MAUREEN No, I've said, I'm waiting for someone.

DINKA Someone else?

MAUREEN Yes.

DINKA Someone particular or just someone?

MAUREEN *(indignantly)* Of course someone particular, what do you think?

DINKA I don't know.

MAUREEN I'm not just sitting here on the off-chance, you know. What do you think I am?

DINKA What time he come?

MAUREEN He was supposed to come half an hour ago.

DINKA What he look like?

MAUREEN He's – he's... I'm not sure. I haven't – Well actually, if you must know I have never met him before. But he should be wearing a flower like this one...

DINKA *(his suspicions confirmed)* Uh-huh.

MAUREEN It's perfectly proper, there's nothing...

DINKA All right. You behave. You cause trouble, I fetch Mr Calvinu, OK? You go out in the road rightaway.

MAUREEN Listen, pigface, don't be so sodding rude, all right? Why don't you just go and—

DINKA *(holding up a warning finger)* Behave!

He exits.

MAUREEN *(draining her glass, muttering)* Right, that's it. I'm not staying in this place. If he can't be bothered to turn up, that's it.

She is about to rise when ADAM *enters. He carries a folder.*

ADAM *(seeing her)* Ah!

MAUREEN *(seeing him)* Oh!

For the ensuing dialogue, MAUREEN *makes a marked effort to "improve" her speech.*

ADAM Hallo.

MAUREEN Hallo.

ADAM Are you who I think you are? Miss—?

MAUREEN *(overlapping)* Yes, yes. You'll be—?

ADAM Yes. Sorry, am I late?

MAUREEN Well, a little bit—

ADAM I am sorry. Not a good start. Sorry. *(He extends his hand)* Adam.

MAUREEN Adam?

ADAM Yes.

MAUREEN I thought you were Robin?

ADAM Robin? No, Adam.

MAUREEN Adam?

ADAM Yes.

MAUREEN Yes. Right. *(She holds out her hand)* I'm Mo'reen...

ADAM Sorry? Marine?

MAUREEN No, Mo'reen...

ADAM Oh, Mo'reen. Yes, right. Should we sit down?

MAUREEN Yes, of course.

> *They both sit.* ADAM *opens his folder and looks at the first sheet.*

ADAM So that's how you pronounce it, is it? Mo'reen?

MAUREEN Yes. Usually, yes.

ADAM *(reading)* M-Y-F-A-N-W-Y. Mo'reen. Unusual.

MAUREEN Pardon?

ADAM That's the correct Welsh way, is it?

MAUREEN Welsh way? What Welsh way?

ADAM In Welsh. You are Welsh, I take it? With a name like Mo'reen – I'd have guessed you were Welsh.

MAUREEN No.

ADAM What are you then?

MAUREEN My father is Irish. Through and through. And my mother is very slightly French.

ADAM I see. *(He is perplexed)*

Slight pause.

MAUREEN My father's a racing driver.

ADAM Goodness.

MAUREEN Formula One.

ADAM How exciting.

MAUREEN Worrying, sometimes.

ADAM Yes. Must be. Especially for your mother.

MAUREEN Yes.

Slight pause.

She's an ex-ballet dancer.

ADAM Sorry? A what?

MAUREEN An ex-ballet dancer...

ADAM Oh, ex-ballet dancer, yes. Sorry, I thought you said an ex-belly dancer. *(He laughs)*

MAUREEN *(smiling, unamused)* No.

ADAM Yes. I'm sorry, I had completely the wrong picture of you in my head. From the description I was given of you.

MAUREEN Description? Oh, you mean the print-out?

ADAM The what?

MAUREEN The computer print-out. You got one on me, did you?

ADAM No.

MAUREEN I got one on you.

ADAM Did you?

MAUREEN Nothing personal. Just the broad details. Mind you, half of them were wrong. I don't think I'd have recognized you, either.

ADAM No?

MAUREEN You weren't even wearing your flower, were you?

ADAM *(completely lost)* No.

MAUREEN I suppose if you'd been smoking your pipe I might have recognized you, I suppose.

ADAM My pipe?

MAUREEN Yes.

ADAM I don't smoke a pipe.

MAUREEN Well, they've certainly got it wrong, haven't they?

> **DINKA** *enters with a menu.*

DINKA You want to order?

ADAM Well, I think we might like a drink first, mightn't we?

DINKA *(recognizing* **ADAM***)* Oh, 's you.

ADAM Yes. Good-evening.

DINKA You with *her*?

ADAM Yes.

DINKA *(to* **MAUREEN***)* You find someone, then?

ADAM What? What's he saying?

MAUREEN *(coolly)* I've no idea what he's saying.

DINKA *(to* **MAUREEN***)* You got lucky, eh?

ADAM I'm sure you'd like another drink? What's that you're having?

MAUREEN This? Oh, this is just tonic water, thank you.

DINKA Tonic water. Cheap.

ADAM Well, I think we should have something a bit more... What about—? What could we have? Kir Royale, perhaps?

MAUREEN Kir...?

ADAM Yes, come on, why not?

MAUREEN All right.

ADAM Two Kir Royale.

DINKA Two Kir Royale. You buying Kir Royale for *her*?

ADAM Yes.

DINKA *(shrugging)* Two Kir Royale...

   DINKA *exits.*

ADAM Do you know him? That waiter?

MAUREEN I certainly don't...

ADAM Funny, he seems to know you. Odd. Anyway. A little bit about me, shall I? While we're waiting. I mean, you've already told me something about you – and anyway – as you're probably aware – you've already got quite a reputation within the business, anyway.

MAUREEN Pardon?

ADAM Well, in your own field. You must be conscious of that. I mentioned your name to one or two close colleagues, they were really impressed—

MAUREEN Colleagues?

ADAM Anyway. Briefly. This is the set-up. Basically, there are the four of us—

MAUREEN Four?

ADAM All together in the same room. Practically in each other's laps.

MAUREEN Laps?

ADAM It's a madhouse. Not the sort of set-up you're used to, I'm sure?

MAUREEN No, not at all.

ADAM And we all need looking after in our different ways. Though hopefully not all at once. Well, not that often. We'd all have call on your services, we'd all have access to your expertise...

MAUREEN Just a minute. Let's get this clear. Are we talking about you and three others?

ADAM Yes. Is that a problem?

MAUREEN Three other men?

ADAM Oh, no, no, no. I thought I explained. There's me. And Daniel, who's overall in charge. And then there's Patricia – Trish – and then there's Carmen who deals with the advertising.

MAUREEN Women as well?

ADAM Yes.

MAUREEN You're joking.

ADAM What is it? Do you not work well with women?

MAUREEN I bloody don't.

ADAM *(dismayed)* Oh. Oh, God. That is a drawback. I had no idea.

MAUREEN What's supposed to happen, then? You two men stand watching, I suppose...

ADAM What?

MAUREEN While we three get down to it? That the idea?

ADAM No. Not at all. God, no, we all muck in together. There's none of that male-female business – not in that place. If something needs doing, whoever's free, they get stuck in and get on with it.

MAUREEN *gets up.*

Where are you going...?

MAUREEN *(coldly)* Good night.

ADAM Just a minute, don't you—

MAUREEN Thank you so much. No, thanks. Goodbye.

MAUREEN *stalks out. She passes* DINKA, *who is carrying a tray with the two glasses of Kir. He stares after* MAUREEN.

ADAM *stands bemused.*

ADAM Where is she—? What have I—?

DINKA She gone?

ADAM Yes. I think so, she – I don't quite know why. She... Why did she walk out like that? Have you any idea?

DINKA *(helpfully)* You didn't offer enough money, who knows?

ADAM No, we never got round to the salary. It wasn't money.

DINKA Who knows? You want this Kir?

ADAM *(consulting his file)* She wrote to me in reply to the ad, she said, she was fed up with working for the big boys, she wanted something more challenging and this job sounded like fun...

DINKA Who knows? Who knows with those women? You're better off without her. I tell you. You get yourself a nice clean girl, eh?

ADAM A nice clean girl?

DINKA From a good house.

ADAM She's not a – nice girl...

DINKA *laughs hollowly.*

No?

DINKA She take all your money. What she give you? Diseases.

ADAM Diseases?

DINKA A whore is a whore is a whore is a whore, eh?

ADAM A whore? She's a whore? A prostitute?

DINKA She sit for hours. One glass of tonic water. No menu. I know straightaway. I say who you waiting for, she say a man, I say what man, she say I don't know, I know him when I see him, I say watch it or you're out in the gutter, OK? ... She's a whore. We get them. Not often but we get them. Saturday night, we get them. Cold night. No underclothes.

ADAM My God. I've been talking to the wrong woman...

DINKA That's what I'm telling you. You want this other glass?

ADAM No. Yes. Leave it there. Where's the one I'm supposed to meet?

DINKA There's another whore?

ADAM No, no... I'm supposed to be meeting this woman. A business meeting.

> **MAUREEN** *returns. She has her coat on.*

MAUREEN Excuse me. I left my handbag. *(She moves to pick it up)*

DINKA *(confidentially, to* **ADAM***)* Look out, look out. She wants to bargain. She's come back to bargain. Be careful, eh?

ADAM *(to* **DINKA***)* Yes, all right, I... *(To* **MAUREEN***)* Excuse me.

MAUREEN Good night.

ADAM Please. Just a minute. Please. *(Urgently)* Please! I say!

MAUREEN *(stopping and turning to him, reluctantly)* What?

> **DINKA** *shakes his head disapprovingly and goes off muttering.*

ADAM I – er...

MAUREEN *(impatiently)* Yes?

ADAM I apologize. There's been a misunderstanding...

MAUREEN There certainly has. *(Threatening to leave)* Is that it?

ADAM No. Just a second, I – I just wanted to explain. You see, I thought you were someone else – please, won't you have your drink...?

MAUREEN No, thank you.

ADAM I realize, I wasted your time and – your time is – is money and I'm really sorry. You see I was looking for a—

MAUREEN I know what you were looking for...

ADAM I was expecting to interview an office manager—

MAUREEN Dear God! Whatever next, she asked?

ADAM A Miss Llewellyn who was supposed to meet me here.

MAUREEN Do I look as if I was born at lunch time?

ADAM It's true. Absolutely true. Look! *(He thrusts his folder at her)* Look! Look. Please. Please.

Something in his tone makes MAUREEN *look at the folder for a second. Then she studies him.*

The truth. Honestly.

MAUREEN You're either a brilliant liar or you're an idiot.

ADAM I'm – an idiot. Probably. Yes.

MAUREEN Yes. I'm inclined to believe you.

ADAM Thank you. *(He offers for her to sit)* Please. Will you finish your drink?

MAUREEN All right. Just the drink.

ADAM If it's not taking up too much of your time...

MAUREEN What else would I be doing?

She sits. ADAM *follows suit.*

ADAM Good health.

MAUREEN Cheers!

They drink.

It's nice. I've never had this. What is it?

ADAM Well. It's basically champagne.

MAUREEN Champagne? Well. You know how to live, you office managers, don't you?

She smiles at him. He smiles back. Then he frowns suddenly.

ADAM You're so young.

MAUREEN How do you mean?

ADAM I'm sorry. To be – doing – what you're doing...

MAUREEN Doing what?

ADAM Oh, I've no right to lecture you – why don't I mind my own business? – it's your life – your choice, presumably...

MAUREEN My what?

ADAM You want to sell yourself for money to every man who asks you, that's up to you. It just seems to me that—

MAUREEN You're doing it again, aren't you?

ADAM What?

MAUREEN *(loudly, angrily rising)* Look, Clarence, for the forty-ninth time, I am not a tart, all right. I am not a prostitute, a call girl, a street-walker, a topless masseuse or a kinky French teacher. I don't do topless lesbian dancing in mud, leather, rubber or bloody bri-nylon. So you'll have to get your rocks off elsewhere, all right? Now bugger off!

ADAM *has risen in horror and is staring round the restaurant in alarm.*

DINKA *enters swiftly.*

DINKA *(to* MAUREEN*)* All right. I warn you. Out now. Out. None of that in here. Out.

DINKA *grasps* MAUREEN*'s elbow.*

MAUREEN *(wriggling free)* Get your hands off me! What's the matter with this place, you're all raving lunatics—

DINKA Out! I call Mr Calvinu...

ADAM Just a minute! You're not... You're not a – a prostitute—

MAUREEN I've told you, no!

ADAM What are you, then?

MAUREEN I'm a fucking hairdresser, aren't I?

DINKA *(deeply shocked)* Hey! Hey! Hey! Hey! Hey! Now I get the manager.

ADAM Just a minute! Just a minute!

MAUREEN It's all right, don't bother, I'm off.

ADAM Please, please! Wait a minute! *(To* DINKA*)* I will vouch for this lady—

MAUREEN I don't need vouching for!

ADAM For both of us. Please. I vouch for both of us. There's been a terrible misunderstanding—

MAUREEN Another one?

ADAM Yes.

MAUREEN How many more goes do you get?

ADAM No more. *(To* DINKA*)* It's all right. We're all right. Wait a second...

DINKA *(as he goes, muttering)* How long you want me to wait? Till she's naked on the table...?

DINKA *goes off.*

MAUREEN *(making to follow* DINKA*)* I've had a basin full of that one—

ADAM I'm sorry. I don't know how all this happened.

MAUREEN Well, I'm bloody sure I don't.

ADAM Will you sit down again?

MAUREEN What's the point? You're only going to ask me to pose for mucky pictures, I know you are.

ADAM I'm not. I promise.

MAUREEN Listen, I came here tonight because I was computer-dated, matched with a man called Robin who smokes a pipe and likes Stevie Wonder and Billy Joel. And he didn't sound like much, but he sounded better than nothing. So I put on my most boring clothes and I came out for a really boring evening. But at least I was going out somewhere because I couldn't stand another Saturday night at home without going raving mad. But I didn't come out for all this. God almighty!

ADAM Oh, that's – I feel so awful about this. Look, we'll try and find this man of yours, shall we? Robin. He's probably sitting waiting here somewhere—

MAUREEN What are you talking about? He'll have run a mile by now, won't he? With his Billy Joel under his arm and his pipe blazing... *(She digs out a card from her handbag)* Look. *(She shows* ADAM*)* Robin Diddswell – The Espresso...

ADAM The Espresso?

MAUREEN That's what it says.

ADAM That's not this place... This is Essa de Calvi. The Espresso is further along.

MAUREEN It is?

ADAM About a hundred yards.

MAUREEN I wondered why he hadn't reserved.

ADAM The Espresso's a wine bar.

MAUREEN A wine bar?

ADAM Quite good soup. Sandwiches.

MAUREEN Soup and sandwiches?

ADAM Well, he may have been planning to go on from there...

MAUREEN No. That doesn't sound like Robin somehow, does it?

ADAM Would you – care to... Perhaps? With me?

MAUREEN Well. *(She considers)* What about your friend?

ADAM I think she's probably fled as well.

MAUREEN Never know her luck. She may end up listening to Billy Joel—

ADAM Choking to death on pipe smoke—

MAUREEN Right.

They smile at each other.

In that case, yes. Thank you very much.

ADAM Good.

They sit.

MAUREEN But we go dutch, all right?

ADAM Well, we'll see. Whatever, it's clearly understood. Just the meal. Nothing else. No strings. No obligations. Right?

MAUREEN Right. No strings...

They smile at each other again as the lights fade on them. The lights rise on the main area. It is a few minutes later. **GERRY** *rises.* **LAURA** *remains seated. She is dozing gently.*

GERRY Right. You ready for off?

LAURA *(starting awake)* What? What's the time?

GERRY Just gone one.

He starts to help gather up her presents, in particular her clock.

LAURA I dozed off, I think.

GERRY Soon be home.

LAURA Now, you're positive you can drive?

GERRY *(lifting the clock)* I can drive... God, this is a weight.

LAURA I said it was. Damn stupid thing to give anyone. Now, I don't want you falling asleep—

GERRY I'm not going to fall asleep. Come on! Shift yourself...

LAURA I need my coat...

They start to leave.

You got the cloakroom ticket?

GERRY Yes. There's not a lot left in there, though. They shouldn't have trouble finding it.

LAURA You still need the ticket—

GERRY I've got the bloody ticket, I've just said I have, woman—

LAURA *(rather wearily)* Don't shout at me, Gerry, don't shout, there's no need to shout at me, is there...?

They have gone.

The lights fade on the main table and come up again on GLYN *and* STEPHANIE's *table, downstage right. (NB: At this stage the main table should be set with clean cutlery, crockery, etc., ready for the last scene on p. 126) It is Tuesday, 16th November, almost two years now since the birthday dinner. For once,* GLYN *is the one seated alone. He appears to have all but finished his meal. He looks at his watch rather anxiously. He seems somehow flabbier both physically and mentally. He sips his coffee.*

In a moment, **STEPHANIE** *arrives. Her image has changed dramatically since we last saw her. She has slimmed right down and is thinner than we have ever seen her, almost gaunt. There is a new-found inner determination about her. Someone who's been through personal crisis and survived. She stands by the table.*

GLYN *does not see her immediately. When he does look up he doesn't, at first, recognize her.*

STEPHANIE *(smiling)* Hi...

GLYN *looks up and stares at her.*

Hallo, Glyn.

GLYN Steph? Hallo. I thought for a minute you weren't—

STEPHANIE Sorry. Things piled up. Have you got long?

GLYN *(nervously)* Well, I have to be... I have to be back by two, actually. I – Never mind, we have twenty minutes. Do you want to eat? Do you want to order? Waiter! I'm afraid, I have started. Well, as you can see I've finished, actually—

STEPHANIE I don't want anything to eat...

GLYN You won't?

STEPHANIE I don't bother much with lunch these days. I'll have a glass of water...

GLYN Waiter! You ought to eat lunch, you know...

STEPHANIE I find I don't need it.

GLYN Well, you look – great. You look really good.

STEPHANIE Thank you. Lost a bit of weight. How are you?

GLYN Oh, I'm fine. *(Calling)* Waiter! *(To her)* I'm still with Barry. Helping Barry out. He needed a hand. It's good. It's a good feeling. Getting shot of all that responsibility. At least temporarily. Working for somebody else. Let them worry about it, eh? For a change?

STEPHANIE *(smiling)* Yes.

GLYN So. Back on the road. Never thought I'd do that again. That's how I started for Dad, you know. Trudging the streets with a sample case. Well, trudging the streets in a company car...

He laughs. He is very nervous and unsure. She smiles.

STEPHANIE *(calling)* Waiter!

TUTO *arrives like a shot.*

TUTO Madametta? What can I—? *(He recognizes* STEPHANIE*)* Madama! It's you!

STEPHANIE Yes.

TUTO Fantastical. You look fantastical. Does she not look fantastical?

GLYN Yes, indeed. I was—

TUTO *(approvingly)* Mmm! Mmm! Like a fashion model. You light up the restaurant.

STEPHANIE *(only slightly embarrassed)* Thank you.

TUTO It's a long time. One year. No?

STEPHANIE Nearly that...

TUTO What can I get you? Some menus? Maybe the sweet trolley, eh?

STEPHANIE *(smiling)* No, not the sweet trolley.

TUTO No sweet trolley?

STEPHANIE No. Just a bottle of water, please. Still water.

TUTO Just a water. Seerar?

GLYN Yes, I'll have another coffee. Black...

TUTO Straight away.

TUTO *goes off.*

STEPHANIE This place is as busy as ever.

GLYN Yes. It's had its ups and downs but—

STEPHANIE I haven't been in here for ages. Must be a year. Nothing's changed. I don't think it's even been repainted.

GLYN Well, old man Calvinu's been laid up recently—

STEPHANIE Oh, dear. Serious?

GLYN Heart, I think. He's taking it easier. He isn't quite so much in evidence these days. What's all that about the sweet trolley...?

STEPHANIE Nothing. Private joke.

GLYN Oh.

TUTO returns with a bottle of water and a glass on the tray.

TUTO *(setting it down by* STEPHANIE*)* 'Scoos. One water.

STEPHANIE No, I'm sorry, that's fizzy water. I asked for still water.

TUTO Sorry?

STEPHANIE I asked for still water. Not fizzy. I don't want this.

TUTO Sorry. Madama. A million pardons. Still water, of course. *(He whisks the bottle and glass away)* 'Scoos. Five seconds. Coffee is coming.

TUTO goes off again.

GLYN So. You've – you've met someone?

STEPHANIE Yes. I've met someone.

GLYN Good, good. Serious? I mean is it...?

STEPHANIE I hope it is. I've agreed to move in with him. With the kids. He's divorced, on his own. No children. So...

GLYN What does he do?

STEPHANIE He's a surgeon. An orthopaedic surgeon.

GLYN *(impressed)* Oh—

STEPHANIE This is why I wanted to meet really. We could have done it all by letter but—

TUTO *arrives again, this time with a bottle of still water and a glass on a tray.*

TUTO Madama. Still water.

STEPHANIE Thank you.

TUTO Coffee's just coming...

TUTO *goes off again.*

STEPHANIE Listen, I know you haven't got much time, so – The point is, I think I would like a divorce. I know you've always said, let's not make irreversible decisions, let's leave things unresolved just in case we decide to... Well, let's be honest, it's not going to happen is it, Glyn—

GLYN I don't know, it—

STEPHANIE Well, it isn't. Not from my side. Not now. It's too late. We've moved on. We both have. All I'm saying is, let's tidy things up, shall we? I think – I probably will remarry sooner or later – For the kids. No, not just for the kids but – And then there's you and Sarah, isn't there? How does she feel about this arrangement? Dragging on? I'm sure she'd like it tidied up, wouldn't she? I can't believe she wouldn't... Surely?

A pause.

So? What do you say? It makes sense, doesn't it?

GLYN *does not reply.*

Glyn? It does, doesn't it? Really? Yes?

GLYN *nods.*

OK. Well. That's all I came to say, really. *(She looks at her watch)* I ought to – I ought to get on... *(Gently)* It's best. Honestly, it is.

GLYN Would you – would you do something for me?

STEPHANIE What?

GLYN Could you – write to my mother – I'm not suggesting you go and see her – just write and say that you're the one who asked for the divorce. Not me.

STEPHANIE You want me to write and tell her that?

GLYN Would you mind?

STEPHANIE I don't mind. OK.

GLYN She might believe it if you – You see before Dad died I made him a promise that, for Mother's sake, I wouldn't, you know, I wouldn't – walk out on you all, you know... I mean I know I haven't been actually living with you, but I haven't walked out on you, have I? Not technically. I've still been looking after you. From a distance. If you appreciate the distinction.

STEPHANIE Your mother may live in a world of her own these days, but I think she might have seen through that, Glyn—

GLYN Please, you will write to her, won't you?

STEPHANIE I've said I will.

GLYN And if you ever feel you can face her for half an hour, she'd love to see the kids again. She really would—

STEPHANIE Oh, Glyn—

GLYN It'd mean so much to her, you know—

STEPHANIE She doesn't want to see them, Glyn. She's not even interested in them.

GLYN Oh, she is, she—

STEPHANIE The only thing that interests her is her. Her and all those bloody dogs she keeps adopting. How many has she got now, five, isn't it?

GLYN Six.

STEPHANIE Six. For God's sake. She's turned that house into a kennels.

GLYN She'd still love to see Tim and Jess—

STEPHANIE Glyn, get it through your head – she doesn't care about you or me – or Sarah or the kids... She is not interested. She is a selfish, self-centred, destructive old woman and she's not worth ruining your life for. Forget about us two, you and me, we're history. Start again, live your own life and to hell with her – marry Sarah, have fifteen kids. Your mother's not worth it. She doesn't love you. She doesn't love anybody except herself, all right?

GLYN She loves Adam.

STEPHANIE I even doubt that, you know.

GLYN Oh, no. She loves Adam. She may not love me. I know she doesn't. But she loves Adam.

STEPHANIE You know what I heard the other day? I was in the hairdressers. My regular one was off sick and guess who I got instead? Maureen. Remember, that girl of Adam's he was so keen on? And, do you know what she told me? Why Adam stopped seeing her? Apparently your mother told him that Maureen's behaviour on her birthday evening upset his father so deeply, that was the reason he got drunk and drove off the road.

GLYN I don't believe it. Mother would never have said that.

STEPHANIE Maybe not, I don't know. Anyway, Maureen's all right. Flashing a brand new engagement ring with a diamond the size of a dinner plate. Listen, what's going to happen to Adam? Is he ever going to move out of there? Live on his own again?

GLYN I don't know. I imagine so. I've no idea what he plans to do.

STEPHANIE Well, I've lost touch. He used to ring me but – If you do see him, tell him my advice is to get out from under. I must dash. I don't know where they've gone with your coffee. *(As she rises)* See you soon. I'll keep in touch.

She kisses him, perfunctorily. He remains seated.

GLYN You know – just before you came, I was sitting here and it occurred to me... You remember that night – the last night we were all together as a family – the night before Dad was killed...?

STEPHANIE Yes, it was that same evening. Mother's birthday party—

GLYN And you and I, we were all set to start again – and Adam had his new girl and Mum and Dad looked so happy and well, the point is – I doubt if any of us knew it at the time – it was something Dad said, actually – that was probably one of the best, the happiest moments of our lives. Only the trouble with those sorts of moments is that you seldom ever realize that they are – until they've gone. Do you see? I mean very rarely do you find yourself saying to yourself, I am happy *now*. Sometimes you say, I was happy *then*. Or sometimes even, I will be happy *when*... But rarely do you get to realize it *now*. If you know what I mean.

STEPHANIE *(gently)* It's for the best, Glyn. It really is. Promise. You'll see. Bye, then.

GLYN *(sadly)* Bye.

STEPHANIE *hesitates for a second about leaving him and then hurries away.*

GLYN *remains where he is.*

ADAM, *dressed as a waiter, enters with a cup of coffee on a tray.*

ADAM Did someone order a black coffee?

GLYN Yes, it's a bit late now, though, I'm— *(He recognizes* **ADAM***)* Oh. Hallo.

ADAM Hi.

GLYN What are you doing?

ADAM I'm working here.

GLYN Since when?

ADAM Since yesterday.

GLYN As a waiter?

ADAM Yes. Mum had a word with old man Calvinu. He said he'd give me a try. It's only temporary, you know. While I get things sorted out. I'm going to night school as well...

GLYN Oh yes? Architecture? Right?

ADAM No, bass guitar...

GLYN Ah.

ADAM You want this coffee?

GLYN It's too late now, I have to go. You were a hell of a time.

ADAM I know. I have trouble working the machine. It's only my second day.

GLYN Yes.

ADAM Do you want it then? Only I can't take it back.

GLYN No, I don't want it.

ADAM You'll have to pay for it.

GLYN I'm not paying for it, I don't want it.

ADAM Oh.

> **GLYN** *gets up.*

How's Sarah?

GLYN Who?

ADAM Sarah? I presume that was Sarah who left?

GLYN No. That was Stephanie.

ADAM Steph! I didn't recognize her. How is she?

GLYN She's – well.

ADAM I haven't talked to her for ages. Well, I don't get much chance these days. Soon as I get home, there's all Mother's dogs to feed, take for walks... All go, eh?

GLYN *(smiling, feebly)* Yes.

ADAM Are you – are you thinking of getting together with Steph again, then?

GLYN No.

ADAM Ah. Sticking with Sarah?

GLYN No, I'm not with Sarah, either.

ADAM Oh. What happened?

GLYN What usually happens, Adam. She went her way, I went mine...

ADAM Yes. That's what usually happens. Except for Mum and Dad. They stuck it out.

GLYN Yes, well. They were exceptional, weren't they? *(He makes to leave)* Look, you drink that. I have to go.

ADAM You want your bill?

GLYN I'll get it at the desk. See you around.

ADAM Yes. Sure.

GLYN *goes off.*

ADAM *has picked up the still full coffee cup and stands uncertainly with it.*

Anyone want a coffee? Black coffee, going spare. Anyone want a coffee...?

He exits.

The lights crossfade to the main table. We are back to the night of the party, at the very start of the evening.

CALVINU *leads* GERRY *and* LAURA *into the room.*

CALVINU   ...through here, please. Tonight we have put you through here—

GERRY This is all for us, is it?

CALVINU Oh yes, all for you. It's suitable?

GERRY Oh, it's fine—

LAURA Yes, we've been in here before. For Adam's twenty-first...

CALVINU For the twenty-first, I remember. And tonight it is your birthday, Laura. I wish you many, many happy returns of the day.

LAURA Thank you.

CALVINU I must apologize, I will be a little absent for some of the evening. We have a big, big party upstairs – they won't disturb you. If I may, I will join you later to drink your health, Laura. I will leave you in the hands of Tuto, you know him, he's my head waiter, he's very, very good—

GERRY Yes, of course we know Tuto...

CALVINU Everything you want, ask him please. Meanwhile I will see your guests are shown through and I will send through the cocktails. Have a happy evening and a successful birthday party, OK?

LAURA Thank you.

GERRY Thank you, Ernesto.

CALVINU *goes off.*

GERRY *waits restlessly whilst* LAURA *inspects the table and the place settings.*

LAURA They've put you at this end, is that all right?

GERRY Fine.

LAURA You wouldn't prefer that other end?

GERRY Makes no difference to me.

LAURA I could swap you round. Put you at that other end.

GERRY No, don't bother...

LAURA It's no bother.

GERRY I'm perfectly happy at that end. Leave it alone.

Pause.

LAURA Sometimes you like to face the window, that's all.

GERRY There's no point in facing the window, is there? It's pitch dark and the curtains are drawn.

LAURA Suit yourself.

Pause.

GERRY Do you want to?

LAURA What?

GERRY Swap round. Go that end?

LAURA No. I don't want to swap ends. Why should I want to swap ends? Makes no difference to me where I sit. *(She studies the table again)* I've put that girl next to you here.

GERRY What girl?

LAURA Adam's girl – *(She strains to read the card)* Maureen, that's her name. Doesn't sound so promising, does it?

GERRY We're reserving judgement now, aren't we?

LAURA Yes... Well, I hope Stephanie's got a new line in conversation, that's all I can say. If she talks babies all evening, I'll throttle her—

GERRY Come on, it's your birthday. Don't get off on the wrong foot—

LAURA It's all right for you—

GERRY She thinks you're interested.

LAURA Why should I be interested...?

GERRY You're Timmy's grandmother, they're very proud of him. They think you'll be proud of him, too... It's sort of natural, you know.

LAURA I still don't see why we should have to talk about him all evening. God, she's a boring girl, isn't she? What a bore? Only someone like Glyn could put up with her—

GERRY *(loudly)* Ah! Here they are...

STEPHANIE *comes in, as at the start of the play. She carries a small gift-wrapped parcel – the ear-rings.*

STEPHANIE Hallo!

LAURA Hallo! Come in...

They kiss.

STEPHANIE Happy birthday, then.

LAURA Thank you.

STEPHANIE Here you are. Little something.

LAURA Oh, bless you. You shouldn't...

STEPHANIE Glyn's got something for you as well. A bigger something. He's just dealing with the coats. *(She moves to* GERRY*)* Hallo, Gerry...

They kiss.

GERRY Hallo, Steph. How are you? How's Timmy, then?

STEPHANIE Oh, he's well. He's bonny. I brought you the new pictures. Just had them developed.

GERRY Oh, grand...

LAURA Lovely.

GERRY You look good.

STEPHANIE Well. I feel good. I feel much better.

GERRY Yes. We're both...you know...thrilled you're—

Before he can continue, **GLYN** *enters boisterously. He carries a large wrapped gift – the clock.*

GLYN Hallo, hallo. Are we in here tonight, are we?

LAURA Yes, they've got a do upstairs apparently. Hallo, dear.

GLYN Hallo, Mum. *(He kisses her proffered cheek)* Happy birthday. Here. Something for you. Look out, it's a bit of a weight.

LAURA *(trying to take it)* Oh, Glyn, it's terribly heavy. I can't possibly hold that, don't be so silly. Put it on the table.

GLYN *(doing so)* I think you'll like it. *(To* **STEPHANIE***)* I think she'll like it, don't you?

STEPHANIE She'll love it. It's brilliant. He picked it all by himself. I had nothing to do with it.

LAURA Where's Adam? I hope he's not going to be late as usual.

STEPHANIE Is he bringing his new girl?

LAURA Yes, whatsername...

GERRY Maureen.

LAURA Maureen. She's a hairdresser, apparently.

STEPHANIE Oh, right. Useful. Must give her a try, mustn't we?

GERRY Where's the bloke with those cocktails? I asked them to bring them through. Cocktails the minute we arrive, I said.

GLYN Want me to check?

GERRY No, it's all right I'll— *(He sees more guests)* Ah. Come in, come in...

LAURA Oh, here they are.

> **ADAM** *enters with* **MAUREEN**, *dressed as at the start of the play.*

ADAM Hallo.

STEPHANIE Hallo.

GLYN Hallo.

MAUREEN *(shyly)* Hallo.

ADAM Everyone, this is – this is Maureen. My friend Maureen. Maureen, this is my mother, Laura.

LAURA *(with great charm)* Hallo, Maureen.

MAUREEN Hallo.

ADAM This is my father...

GERRY Hallo, Maureen, I'm Gerry...

MAUREEN How do you do...

ADAM My brother, Glyn...

GLYN Hallo.

MAUREEN Hallo.

ADAM And last but not least, this is my sister-in-law, Stephanie...

STEPHANIE Hallo, Maureen, good to meet you...

MAUREEN Nice to meet you. Thank you.

> *A brief silence. They all look at* **MAUREEN** *but no one speaks.* **MAUREEN** *is aware she is somewhat over-dressed. She smiles as best she can.*

GERRY Well. All met. Shall we all sit down? I think we've got our places marked for us, haven't we? Maureen, I'm afraid you're stuck this end next to me.

MAUREEN Right. Thank you.

TUTO *enters with a tray of champagne cocktails.*

GERRY And, Steph, you're the other side of me here... Ah, Tuto, at last. Where have you been, feller?

TUTO I'm sorry, I'm sorry. With the champagne, it's not good to open to the last minute. *(To* **LAURA***)* Madama, a cocktail?

LAURA Thank you, I'm gasping for something.

GERRY *(under this last, to* **MAUREEN***)* I could open a bottle of champagne a damn sight quicker than this lot...

MAUREEN *laughs.*

TUTO *(continuing, uninterrupted)* Madama, happy birthday.

LAURA Thank you.

TUTO *(to* **ADAM***)* Seerar?

ADAM *(accepting his drink)* Thank you.

STEPHANIE *(as* **TUTO** *continues round the table, to* **MAUREEN***)* Did you come by taxi?

MAUREEN No, we walked.

TUTO *(giving a glass to* **STEPHANIE***)* Madama...

STEPHANIE *(to* **TUTO***)* Thank you. *(To* **MAUREEN***)* Walked? That's noble.

MAUREEN I don't live too far away.

GERRY Whereabouts do you live?

TUTO *(to* **GERRY***)* Mr Stratton.

GERRY Thank you.

MAUREEN Harwick Road. It's just off North—

TUTO *(to* MAUREEN*)* Madametta?

MAUREEN Thank you.

GERRY Oh yes, we know Harwick Road—

LAURA Oh, yes. Don't we have warehouses somewhere round there?

TUTO *(serving* GLYN *last)* Seerar.

GLYN Thank you.

GERRY Yes, we do... We have our paint store down there—

ADAM Maureen lives the other end. By the canal.

LAURA Oh, in one of those lovely little cottages?

MAUREEN Yes.

LAURA By the canal?

MAUREEN Yes.

LAURA Lovely old places. Aren't they damp, at all?

MAUREEN No, not really, no.

LAURA Amazing. I'd have thought being that near water. *(To* STEPHANIE*)* I don't think I could live near canals. I'd be frightened of rats and things, wouldn't you?

STEPHANIE Well—

MAUREEN We don't have rats—

ADAM They don't have rats, Mother—

LAURA Oh really. I thought that's where rats lived. Near canals—

ADAM Mother—

MAUREEN They can live anywhere. Can rats.

LAURA Really?

MAUREEN Wherever there's dirt. Or filth. Or any sort of shit for that matter.

A brief pause.

GERRY *(smoothing things over)* Well, I think a little toast is in order. I don't want to make a long speech but... Just to say, happy birthday to Laura. And to thank her for putting up with me for another year... And here's to many more of those. I'd just like to add, it's very nice to see us all together as family – Glyn and Steph – and Adam – and to welcome Maureen. I hope we'll be seeing a lot more of you, Maureen.

STEPHANIE *(kindly)* Hear! Hear!

MAUREEN *gives her a smile of gratitude.*

GERRY And without getting philosophic – which as you know isn't my way—

LAURA *gives a short ironic laugh.*

Nevertheless – you know, in life, you get moments – just occasionally which you can positively identify as being among the happy moments. They come up occasionally, even take you by surprise, and sometimes you're so busy worrying about tomorrow or thinking about yesterday that you tend to miss out on them altogether. I'd like to hope tonight might be one such moment. And if it is – let's not miss out on this one, all right? All that really means is, enjoy yourselves. *(Slight pause)* Anyway. To Laura and – to happy times.

They all rise, except for **LAURA,** *and raise their glasses.*

ALL *(except* **LAURA***)* To Laura...happy times...

LAURA *(still seated, murmuring)* Happy times...

They drink. **MAUREEN** *alone remains standing after they are seated, draining her glass.*

MAUREEN *(banging down her glass rather noisily)* Lovely.

She smiles at them all. She realizes she is the only one still standing and sits. As she does so, the lights fade to a blackout.

FURNITURE AND PROPERTY LIST

ACT I

On stage: Main table, centre, with 6 chairs. *On it:* place-names, used coffee-cups, dirty plates, sweet-papers, ashtrays, liqueur glasses, gift wrapping, cutlery, crockery, etc.

Table for two, downstage left. *On it:* cutlery, crockery, etc.

Table for two, downstage right. *On it:* cutlery, crockery, etc.

Gifts and wrapping paper (**Laura**)

Large mantelpiece clock

Macramé plant holder

Volume of poetry

"Craft" ear-rings (**Laura**)

Coffee-pot (**Tuto**)

Offstage: Mop and bucket (**Bengie**)

2 glasses of brandy (**Bengie**)

Coffee-pot (**Tuto**)

Coat (**Stephanie**)

Tray. *On it:* whisky, small jug of water, bottle of carbonated water, glass (**Calvinu**)

Menus (**Calvinu**)

2 glasses of brandy (**Gerry**)

Grapefruit cocktail (**Stephanie**)

Glass of scotch and water (**Tuto**)

Plate of pasta (**Tuto**)

Paper hats (**Adam** and **Maureen**)

Sweet trolley. *On it:* sweets, crockery, etc. (**Aggi**)

Tray. *On it:* 3 small glasses and bottle of fine liqueur (Schroopellick) (**Calvinu**)

Personal: **Maureen:** handbag. *In it:* macramé plant holder, identical to the one set on stage

ACT II

Set: Half-bottle of liqueur on main table
Cutlery, crockery, drinks, food (fish, meat), etc. on table downstage left
Menu, cutlery, crockery, flowers in vase, drinks (mineral water), food (salad), etc. on table downstage right

Offstage: Chopped fruit (**Maureen**)
Soup (**Adam**)
Filofax (**Glyn**)
Sweet trolley. *On it:* sweets, cutlery, crockery, etc.
Red flower (**Maureen**)
Menus (**Dinka**)
Folder (**Adam**)
Tray. *On it:* two glasses of Kir Royale (**Dinka**)
Coat (**Maureen**)
Coffee-cup (**Glyn**)
Tray. *On it:* bottle of water and glass (**Tuto**)
Still water (**Tuto**)
Tray. *On it:* coffee-cup (**Adam**)
Wrapped parcel (**Stephanie**)
Large wrapped gift (**Glyn**)
Tray. *On it:* champagne cocktails (**Tuto**)

Personal: **Adam**: box. *In it:* engagement ring
Maureen: handbag
Stephanie: handbag. *In it:* postcard
Laura: handbag

Note: During the lighting change on p. 116, the main table must be re-set with cutlery, crockery, place-names, etc. Flip-top tables may help to facilitate this and all other layout changes.

LIGHTING PLOT

Practical fittings required: nil

Interior. The same throughout

To open: Main table, centre, visible with slightly under-lit
restaurant lighting

ACT I

Cue 1	**Laura:** "I never realized we were in trouble..." *Crossfade to downstage right corner table; keep dim light on Gerry and Laura at main table*	(Page 28)
Cue 2	**Glyn:** "...what are you going to have then?" *Crossfade to main table*	(Page 37)
Cue 3	**Laura:** "Don't order anything for me, will you..." *Crossfade to downstage left corner table*	(Page 39)
Cue 4	**Adam:** "...like that in front of them, will you?" *Crossfade to main table*	(Page 45)
Cue 5	**Laura:** "Thanks a bunch." *Crossfade to table downstage right*	(Page 46)
Cue 6	**Stephanie:** "Benzay appertass!" *Crossfade to table downstage left*	(Page 53)
Cue 7	**Maureen** grabs **Adam**'s sweet bowl and starts eating *Crossfade to main table*	(Page 59)
Cue 8	**Calvinu:** "...to the wisdom of the wine." *Dim a little, but not entirely, on main table and bring up lights on table downstage left*	(Page 63)

EFFECTS PLOT

ACT I

Piped music of indeterminate ethnic origin is heard from time to time throughout the scenes at the main table

No cues

ACT II

No cues

THIS IS NOT THE END